CUT-and-SLASH
BASKETBALL

CUT-and-SLASH BASKETBALL

Robert T. Samaras

PARKER PUBLISHING COMPANY, INC.
West Nyack, New York

© 1974 *by*

PARKER PUBLISHING COMPANY, INC.

West Nyack, N.Y.

Library of Congress Cataloging in Publication Data

Samaras, Robert T
    Cut-and-slash basketball.

    SUMMARY: Discusses the strategy and techniques of an
offensive basketball system based on the concept of main-
taining constant pressure on the defense regardless of
type.
    1. Basketball--Offense. [1. Basketball--Offense]
I. Title.
GV889.S19   796.32'32   74-8347
ISBN 0-13-196592-1

Printed in the United States of America

I would like to dedicate this book to the beautiful women in my life—my wife Marietta and daughters Debra, Nikki, and Valeri—a feminine movement whose prime objective has been to serve as my most devoted, dedicated, and faithful boosters, sharing the joys of victory while easing the pain of defeat. Sweethearts—I thank you.

A Word About This Versatile Offense for Winning Basketball

The Cut-and-Slash Offense is a multipurpose offense, a brand of basketball that is fast and that opens numerous avenues to scoring. The attack puts pressure on the defense and exploits any weakness that may be prevalent. Then the offensive team has various movements to select from to take advantage, making it possible to attack and exploit any type of defense at any time during the game.

I have always been completely charmed and obsessed by the fast, exciting style of basketball where high scoring reigns supreme. Scoring is fun for players and spectators alike. The Cut-and-Slash is used to take advantage of nearly every conceivable way to make a basket. A unique feature of this offense is that most of the scoring chances are developed close to the basket in high scoring-percentage areas. A team should win a game by outscoring the opposition, rather than by out-defensing the opponent.

My philosophy of Blitz Basketball entails pressing the opposition to gain possession of the ball in order that the offense may apply pressure while scoring more points. Using pressure defense speeds up the game while bringing a devastating force to bear against the opponent's offensive efforts. The Cut-and-Slash complements this philosophy with pressure offensive tactics that overpower the opponent's defense. There are times when control of game tempo is essential, and this also is very feasible with the Cut-and-Slash.

The attack was founded and developed on the basic assumption that more versatile and capable modern players can learn more intricate offensive movements than were possible in the past. The types of drills and the way coaches teach the drills make this learning expedient.

Learning one basic offense with many alternative maneuvers may be adequate for some teams, but the highly successful team must learn a variety of basic plays in order to cope with outstanding opponents. The outstanding team must have in its repertoire, and must practice often, a variety of maneuvers within the realm of basic basketball.

Coaches must do justice to players by helping them develop into complete, well-rounded players capable of executing many moves, shots, rebounding, and other ball-handling techniques. The versatility and dexterity of these players can then be integrated into the team patterns, offering shot possibilities against any defense. With minor adjustments, each pattern must be applicable against basic defenses, half-court pressure defenses, and full-court pressure defenses.

The offense itself is a highlight of this book, but there are also some other novel ideas to consider. First is the balance wheel concept of balancing the floor while making available moves and shots by each player at each spot. Second, the unique transitional free-lance attack adds another dimension to offensive basketball. Third is the four-step approach to each option with the potential continuity of the cuts or of the total option. Fourth is the capability of implementing each option against the various defenses.

Ideas in this book may be quickly incorporated into any team offensive attack, as can the total offense. The drills simplify the implementation of the attack. The method of practicing the drills is significant in terms of the time needed to learn the Cut-and-Slash while deriving its benefits and appreciating its features.

The attack evolved from the thinking of a basketball coach who scouted, researched and experimented with the offense for years during both practices and games. The real value of the attack stems from the fact that many of the ideas have been borrowed from fine coaches throughout the country. Many of these ideas were derived from varied offensive maneuvers which are characteristic of basketball in general. Personal ideas combined with the borrowed ones were integrated into this dynamic attack. The drills which are listed help develop the personnel and mold the players into this all-purpose, multiple attack.

This book will give a step-by-step progression along with methods and techniques necessary to develop the Cut-and-Slash. If the procedures outlined are followed, a team should be able to develop the attack to its fullest in a short time, thus becoming a team capable of playing winning basketball.

Robert Samaras

ACKNOWLEDGMENTS

To Dr. John Telford, Divisional Director of Health, Physical Education and Athletics of the Berkley School System, Berkley, Michigan, in recognition for editing the manuscript.

To Dr. Morrel J. Clute, Professor of Education at Wayne State University, for urging me to write the text, and to Dr. Leon Lande, Associate Professor of Health and Physical Education, for his encouragement.

To the young men I have had the privilege to coach, wherever they may be.

To fellow coaches in Canada and the United States who have always shared their basketball knowledge so willingly with me. Principally to Lou Carnesecca of St. John's University, New York, Ray Mears and Stu Aberdeen from the University of Tennessee, and Bill Gleason from Loyola Academy High School, Winnetka, Illinois.

To Chalmer G. Hixson, Director of the Division of Health and Physical Education at Wayne State University, for giving me the opportunity to become the head basketball coach at my alma mater.

Finally, I would like to pay tribute to my personal friends who have supported our basketball program throughout the years: Dr. Dick Moriarty, Athletic Director at Windsor University; Eddi Chittaro, my fine assistant coach at Windsor University; Ken Fathers, sports writer for the *Windsor Star* Newspaper; Herman L. Masin, Sports Editor for the *Scholastic Coach Magazine*; Gunars Vitolin, Vernon E. Keyes, Christ Petrouleas, Nick Cheolas, Dr. John S. Kastran, Homer (Tip) Smathers, Deno Skuras, Bob Soloman, Peter Bill Sr., George Backos, Bill Kreifeldt, Joel Mason, Betty Smith, Toni Nicholas Allen, Fedon Matheou, Rev. Normand Martin S.M., and the late Harry (Bob) Collins.

Table of Contents

SYMBOLS USED IN DIAGRAMS

1 – 2 – 3 – 4 – 5   Offensive Players

①   Player with Ball

X   Defensive Man

Dribble

Pass (small number indicates number of pass in that sequence)

Movement of Player (small number indicates number of player movement in that sequence)

Screen

Screen and Roll

Change of Pace

Defensive Pinch (or Trap)

⊗   Coach

1

The Cut-and-Slash Attack:
A Pressure Offense

The Cut-and-Slash Attack is a complete offense geared and developed to meet the demands of modern basketball. It is an offense that applies continual pressure in the form of scoring thrusts against any and all basketball defenses. The continual and extensive movements by the offensive team force the defensive team into a multitude of errors. With this pressure offense, the defense can be weakened and forced to crumble. This is characteristic during the game, but particularly in crucial situations, due to the variety of scoring opportunities.

The Cut-and-Slash Attack is a multiple offense. There are several options available to give a wide and diverse effect, giving the offensive team the necessary scope to develop an outstanding dynamic attack. Each option is composed of a progressive four-step dimension which includes ostensibly every imaginable type of offensive manuever. There are individual moves and drives fundamental to each step in every option. This variety of options with the step dimension and inclusive fundamental moves and drives creates a multitude of high percentage shots in close to the basket.

The offense includes all the latest facets in high-powered, high-scoring modern basketball. There are opportunities to use most conceivable maneuvers in this offensive attack because of its multiple nature and modern facets. With only minor adjustments, the Cut-and-Slash Attack can demolish man-to-man defenses, zone defenses, and

17

combination defenses, as well as full-court pressure defenses. Its quick-cutting and hard-slashing types of movements find holes against even the best defensive teams.

Another feature of the attack is that it makes allowances for outstanding offensive players. Although this is a team offense, considerations are made for players with special attributes and outstanding offensive techniques. It is possible to take advantage of the exceptional players' abilities.

EVOLUTION OF THE CUT-AND-SLASH ATTACK

In the beginning stages of the Cut-and-Slash, the attack was basically made up of simple cuts to the basket. The main reason for this simple attack was that cutting was effective enough against the defenses of the day. With the improvement of the defensive aspect in basketball, there was a need for a much more diversified attack. I realized that the offense had to enlarge its scope, that new steps had to be added to the offense to make it more effective. It was apparent that there was a need for secondary attacks, for continuity, for baseline-to-baseline scoring, and for quick changes to meet changing situations in the development of a versatile team offense.

Team offense means the inclusion of all players on the floor in the attack, while developing an offensive thrust to pass the ball to allow a man closest to the basket with the best shot to shoot. One of the characteristics of championship teams that I coached through the years (25 championships in ten years) was the fact that all players were scoring threats. Scoring involved total cooperation in passing, movement, and shooting by all players as a single unit. Teams sharing the ball and sharing responsibilities on offense (and defense) are the teams that win games and championships. An example of this can be shown on every level of basketball, whether it is elementary school, high school, college or professional.

FOUR-STEP ATTACK

The Cut-and-Slash Offense is symbolized by four different dimensions. Actually, each dimension is a step attack and follows a form of progressive continuity. Step 1 in the attack is the *cutting phase*. In the cutting phase the person cutting to the basket is either the ball passer, or one man removed from the passer, or in some cases two men removed from him. The cutter makes a direct line, usually at top speed, to the basket.

Step 2 is the *slashing attack*. This attack is a little different because whereas the cutting phase is more essentially a clean, direct movement to the basket, the slashing attack involves blocking and screening by two or more players to free a shooter. A slasher moves through traffic, and if not clear, he may set up a screen for someone else to slash to the basket. The slashing phase means literally to fight to the basket.

Step 3 is called the *balance wheel*. This has come about through the need for some type of offensive attack to take place if the cutting and slashing was offered an opportunity for a shot. The balance wheel is basically a balancing of the floor with the players by moving to key positions and getting clear to shoot, to drive, or to pass. Many shots may be taken off the balance wheel, since players move to open spots on the floor where players may be left unguarded temporarily. "Find the open man" is the common expression to alert players to pass the ball to an unguarded player.

The *weak-side slash* is Step 4. It follows the balance wheel and leads to individual movements, two-man movements, or three-man movements to clear a player for a lay-up or a jump shot. These movements involve some individual play and general slashes usually generated by passing the ball around the balance wheel to the weak-side area away from where the balance wheel attack originated. Basically these are the four steps involved in Cut-and-Slash offense, and they open up the various scoring opportunities and produce an aggressive, complete offense.

FEATURES OF THE CUT-AND-SLASH OFFENSE

Modern basketball is predicated on the premise of scoring. There are teams built around the theory of ball control, but for the most part these teams are few in number. The emphasis now is on putting many points on the board to win. The Cut-and-Slash offers many benefits to teams desiring to increase scoring capacity. Here are the benefits of the system:

1. Ultra-Modern Offense

The offense is geared to include modern offensive principles and can combat any defense in basketball. This offense can score against any type of defense successfully.

2. Teamwork Approach

Playing this attack involves complete teamwork. Any player may line up at any position for pattern involvement. The attack affords players various movements and allows open players to shoot high percentage shots.

3. Easy-to-Learn Attack

This attack involves use of basic plays developing into more complicated maneuvers. Ideally, the simplicity itself is unique and one of the virtues of the attack.

4. Close-In Shots

This attack offers a variety of shots: first, a lay-up off the cutter; second, a lay-up or hook off the slashers; third, a jump shot from outside or off the balance wheel; and fourth, any assortment or variety of plays of give-and-go or pass and individual moves. These moves make available close to the basket in the internal zone any of the shots mentioned.

5. Exploiting Weak Defensive Player

This offense is geared to find the weak player. If a team is vulnerable due to slow, unskilled personnel, or personnel that cannot react defensively, the offense can run rampant. The defense must be willing to run hard to stay up with the cutters, willing to fight through screens to contain the slashers, and alert at all times to cope with the balance wheel and the weak-side attack. Because of all the movements, there are very few defenses that can contain this complete offense. These hard, direct cuts and slashes to the basket force the defense into making mistakes.

6. Aggressive Offense

The nature of the cuts and slashing movements makes for a very aggressive offense. The players become extremely aggressive and seem to refine quick movements. No defense dares fall asleep against this offense. If a defense is a standing-around type, the moving offense will have a distinct advantage with the rapid maneuverability.

7. Scoring Opportunities for Any Player

The Cut-and-Slash and the variety of movements by each player are conducive to scoring opportunities for all players. Any player moving to the basket can become a scoring threat. If there is no shot, he moves out of the shooting area to make room for another player to enter the scoring area to shoot. If he is not clear, the movement is to get out and allow another player to come in for a shot. The balance wheel offers a shot for any player who is open. If there is still no potential shooter, then the two-man plays start on the weak side. With all these, any player in the clear for shooting may take a shot. The offense is not geared to one shooter. It is not geared for the star to free himself for the shot, but rather for anyone with a good shot to shoot.

8. Taking Advantage of Individual Abilities

Although the Cut-and-Slash is a team offense, there are ways to take advantage of players with individual abilities. For example, a strong inside scorer eventually will have opportunities to use his moves and shots in close to the basket. Excellent jump shooters will have time to shoot their jumper near the basket. Outstanding drivers will have time and opportunities to move to the basket with a drive for a shot. In essence, the outstanding players can and will have opportunities to operate in favorite spots. This is not to say that a coach should look strictly for the star player, but it is vital that players possessing certain abilities have the opportunities to use these abilities along with all the other possibilities.

9. Quick Scoring Thrust

As a coach interested in and thrilled by high scoring, I have always been thrilled by the electrifying type of scoring made possible by the Cut-and-Slash. The thrusts toward the basket are direct, quick, and continual. It is felt that athletes should be shooting within a time span ranging from two to eight seconds after the offense begins. This stresses the theory that the more good shots, the more possibility of scoring. To get into these good shooting positions demands lightning-like thrusts, and this is made possible with the many special designs of the Cut-and-Slash.

10. Attack Presses

The offense is geared to attack aggressively any type of press or presses. We carry the fight to the defense. The plan is to move in for the score from position of the ball in relation to the count. The movements of players offer excellent close-in shots.

11. Demolishing Regular Zone Defenses

The offense offers outstanding opportunities to move inside, through, and around zones. Teams can have a lot of success attacking any and all zones with our clocking movements.

12. Demolishing Stand-Back Basic Zones

One of the key points of the writer's teams' zone offenses is that if a zone stands still (as often happens with high school teams), the attack quickly opens up the door for high percentage shots.

13. Attack from Any Part of the Court

A unique factor of the Cut-and-Slash Attack is that the offense may start from anywhere on the court. In recent years there has been a lot of discussion about baseline-to-baseline offense, and this is due to the numerous pressing teams in the game today. The attack is geared to originate anywhere on the court. The movements are very similar and can be performed immediately after throwing the ball in, or from three-quarter court, from half-court, or from the top of the 21-foot circle. Ideally, the best starting position is just over mid-court against a half-court pressing team. Another good starting point is deep in the back court against the full-court pressure-type teams. Our attack is geared from a set position to move into a regular pattern. This can be extremely effective from anywhere on the court.

14. Excellent Offensive Rebounding Position

Another benefit of the attack is the fact that with the nature and the execution of so many movements, offensive players secure excellent rebounding position. The defense is attacked so aggressively that players are usually moving to the basket. With the quick moves and aggressive blocks, the offensive men are able to slide into excellent rebounding position. The defense can be forced under the basket into a poor rebounding area. The defense can also be forced into each other and get the offense that split-second timing needed to secure strong rebounding position. These tactics have often permitted my teams to out-rebound many bigger opponents.

It has frequently been found that the big teams and the big men do not like to move away from the basket area. Consequently, by drawing these big boys away, my teams have been able to take advantage of their smaller players who may be excellent rebounders. When bigger boys on defense are pulled away from the boards, it seems to confuse many of them. Bigger offensive boys can take advantage and have the edge moving back to the rebounding positions before the defensive man can recover. This is one reason why the balance wheel is so successful. Defensive tall men feel lost on occasion when forced to move away from the backboards. Consequently, with this reluctance they stay in the close range of the basket where they can quickly go in for a rebound. As a result, players moving to the balance wheel increase the opportunity to shoot before the defensive man can react.

15. Building Offensive Momentum

Basketball is a game of momentum, which means that once the scoring begins for a team, that particular team can keep right on scoring in rapid fashion and continue to perpetuate scoring success. This offense is very conducive to building momentum, because its lightning-like thrusts and its continual movement to the basket create many opportunities for scoring. This also influences the psychological outlook of the players, and the momentum crescendoes. Once the attack takes place and becomes successful, players just seem to have that little bit of extra drive necessary to continue building momentum.

16. Allowing for Player Development

In our offense, players have an excellent opportunity of developing due to the great demands of movement in all directions, the versatility of play, and the continuation of action where the player has an opportunity to shoot, pass, or rebound. Because of the long floor movements, players seem to develop physically.

17. Controlling Game Tempo

The offensive movements are such that we can control the game tempo with the offense. Regardless of how much is written about the defense as the controlling force of scoring, the offense is the heart of the attack of a team that controls tempo. It has been found necessary to control the tempo of some rare games. Even with my teams' aggressive style, some bigger and stronger opponents have forced the offense to control the tempo of a game at times. The Cut-and-Slash has many movements facilitating ball control and enabling the offense to control the tempo, while still leaving the door open for scoring.

18. Thrilling the Spectators

People enjoy watching this brand of offense. The fast, daring charge toward the basket with players dashing through various patterns, and the speeded-up, high-scoring tactics of the game have earned this offense its name: the Cut-and-Slash Attack.

Spectators delight in this thrilling style of basketball, and they often help build momentum. The players enjoy playing it and the crowd loves to watch—everyone knows a crowd practically goes wild during extremely high-scoring games! Two characteristics prove the point: first, record crowds have seen my teams play; and second, the crowds have always been extremely enthusiastic and appreciative in response to these basketball teams.

19. Enjoyable Play

A player naturally receives satisfaction from scoring. Players appreciate this all-out attack since each assumes a major role in all offensive aspects. The substitutes are happy because of the chance to play. Each has a chance to play the various positions at times, including the post position, since players become proficient in the area. Players also have ample opportunities to free-lance with individual moves with the ball, particularly off the balance wheel spots.

DISADVANTAGES OF THE ATTACK

A word should be mentioned about the disadvantages or weakness in any attack. The Cut-and-Slash needs players with versatility. It has been proved that boys can be developed to high-skill level with proper drills, especially since the required skills are rather basic. Careless passing and poor timing are anathema to the attack, but these can be pitfalls in any offensive system. None of these weaknesses is insurmountable, and each can be controlled with proper practice.

2

The Four Steps in the
Cut-and-Slash Attack

The Cut-and-Slash Attack revolves around four basic steps, along with variations within each step. The attack basically may be centered around any one of the three lanes of the basketball court. Diagram 2-1 is a description of the lanes and the way one divides the basketball court. The A lane is the left lane, the B lane is in the middle, and the C lane is on the right. Lanes extend from baseline to baseline. Different attacks focus either in the same lane as the ball, in the middle lane, or in the opposite lane of the ball. An attack might initiate in the right lane but end up with scoring taking place in the left lane. The scoring thrusts need not take place in the same lane of the play's origin. The point being made is that in this attack the total floor is utilized to move toward the basket in rapid fashion.

The four steps are important because they give a continuous and planned flow of movements to the attack. With each movement, various scoring opportunities unfold. Scoring evolves around high percentage shots close to the basket. Each step has individual uniqueness designed to take advantage of individual moves or combined player moves in relation to open court areas. Each creates offensive thrusts and pressures the defense with movement patterns geared to penetrate the internal area or to attack outside after forcing the defense to protect the internal zone.

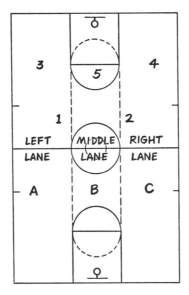

DIAGRAM 2-1
The Three Floor Lanes

These tactics offer an internal offense with inside-out scoring. Shots are set up first close to the basket, then, when the defense adjusts to this maneuver, shots become available from the outside area. Diagram 2-2 outlines the internal zones. Inside-out scoring is available with each of the four steps.

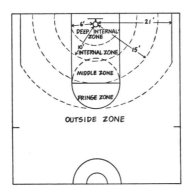

DIAGRAM 2-2
The Shooting Zones

THE FOUR BASIC STEPS

The four steps are: (1) the *cut*, (2) the *slash*, (3) the *balance wheel*, and (4) the *weak-side slash*. Another component is the "continuity characteristic." Continuity enables the offense to begin all over again and run through each step in its proper order. The continuity may be used very effectively when scoring must be from a patient attack tempo. But this is a rarity in our system.

The idea of the Cut-and-Slash is to move to the basket as rapidly as possible in attacking the other team. The four steps which follow can be used in various ways, but basically do follow in unison. Each step is contingent upon the development of the previous one. The cut is the first step. If nothing is developed here, then the slash occurs, followed by the balance wheel. Finally the weak-side slash is available. Each offers a wide range of scoring chances. There is no consistency as to which step is most effective. All are necessary, since each has a definite purpose. If no opportunity presents itself during execution of the four steps (which is unusual), then the move is to form the balance wheel and proceed to the weak-side slash. If necessary, players may keep repeating these two steps.

1. The Cut

Probably the most useful purpose of the cut is to move directly to the basket for a shot, but there are two other facets of this step. First, the cut forces the defense to collapse to the basket, and second, it leads to the second step with the cutter screening for the slasher.

The cut can take various forms. It can be made simply by one player passing the ball from the guard position to the forward, followed by the guard cutting to the basket. He can use either a change of pace, a change of direction, or a series of fakes before making his initial move. The cut may also be made by a player other than the passer. But basically and simply, the cut is the first movement directly, and usually quite rapidly, to the basket.

Diagrams 2-3, 2-4, and 2-5 depict different types of cuts. Diagram 2-3 shows the simple cut with the change of pace and a direct move to the basket for a pass from 4. Movement is away from the ball if the cutter receives no pass. Diagram 2-4 shows a cutter who passes

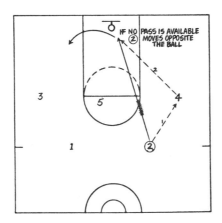

DIAGRAM 2-3
Simple Cut with a Change of Pace

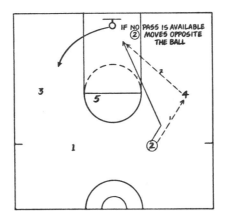

DIAGRAM 2-4
Simple Cut with a Change of Direction

to a forward, begins to break toward the receiver and then suddenly moves directly to the basket to receive a pass from 4. If he does not get the ball for a shot, the move is away from the ball. Diagram 2-5 shows player 2 passing the ball to 4, who makes a series of fakes by going away from the ball temporarily, slowing down, faking toward the ball and then making a direct line to the basket for a pass from 4. If player 2 is not clear for a pass, the player again moves away from the ball.

Using two guards or two forward cutters are other variations. Criss-crossing as well as rubbing off may also take place.

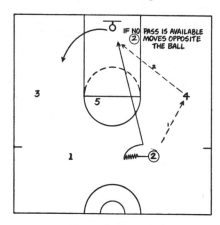

DIAGRAM 2-5
Simple Cut with a Change of Pace and a Change of Direction

2. The Slash

The slash follows the cut. Screen and roll plays characterize the slash. The purpose is to have players interact with screening maneuvers to confuse a man-for-man defense, permitting an offensive player to get free for a shot. The slash is a movement by a player opposite the ball usually, who comes off the cutter and breaks to the basket. The cutter sets up the slash if he was unable to shoot. He slows down just beyond the three-second area and looks to block or screen for a player about to slash to the basket. When this is done, the slasher goes either to the right or to the left of the screen, preceded by a series of fakes, and moves into a shooting zone. There are several different types of slashes. The *simple slash* is where the player basically makes a cut off the moving cutter and goes toward the basket. The object of this is to beat the defensive man to the shooting area or try to force him under the basket. The slasher may receive a pass for a one-on-one situation or a simple lay-up.

The *hook-up* is a similar type of slash, with the exception that the cutter moving off or away from the basket intentionally screens and sets up the forward who is trying to move to the basket by hooking his man up on the screener. The slasher coming in looks for the quick pass for a shot, and if not clear, he goes to the corner while the screener looks to roll back underneath the basket for a quick pass and a lay-up, or a one-on-one situation. The *rub-off* is when a player moving directly to the basket rubs his man off the post man or a forward who is

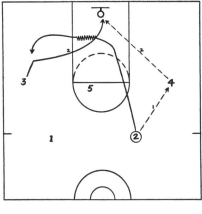

DIAGRAM 2-6
Simple Slash

standing between the foul line extended and the top of the free-throw circle.

The next three diagrams show the different types of slashes. Diagram 2-6 shows the simple slash. In this diagram, offensive man 2 passes to number 4 and breaks directly to the basket. When there is no shot available, he moves out to the opposite side of the pass receiver (4). As 2 passes near the basket he slows down, and 3 slashes off him and moves directly to the basket. In this particular play, number 2 does not return to the basket but continues to a new position.

Diagram 2-7 depicts the hook-up. In this diagram 2 passes to 4,

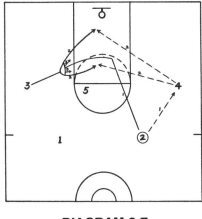

DIAGRAM 2-7
Hook-Up

then breaks to the basket. If he is not clear, he moves to the left side of the basket and picks just outside of the three-second zone. Three tries to hook his man up on 2 and then moves either way to the basket for a pass and shot, or a one-on-one. If 4 is not clear, 3 moves out of the shooting area and 2 makes a reverse pivot and roll move by taking up as much space as possible, then moves into the shooting zone for a pass. The rub-off is a little different from the hook-up, because the rub-off takes place beyond the foul line. Usually the rub-off will take place between the foul line and the free-throw circle or from the foul line extended to the top of the free-throw circle.

Diagram 2-8 shows the rub-off. Two passes to 4, and the man

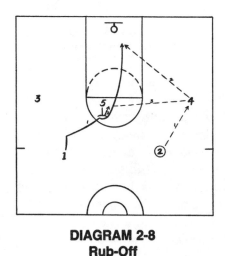

DIAGRAM 2-8
Rub-Off

rubbing off moving to the basket is 1. In this case, 1 is the man away from the ball, which is another characteristic of the rub-off. For example, 1 moves in to rub off his man against 5. The idea is that 1 moves in for the lay-up and if not clear goes away from the ball while 5 screens. If 5 can, he hooks 1's man on his back, pivots and moves in for a lay-up. If not clear, he moves out of the lane in either direction.

One other slash that takes place with a forward-center interchange is shown in Diagram 2-9. This is called the *split-in-and-out*. The diagram illustrates the following: 2 passes to 4. Five screens from a side middle-post position. Three goes off the screen in to the basket while 5 screens and moves out to the free-throw line. (Three could also slash right and 5 would go in.)

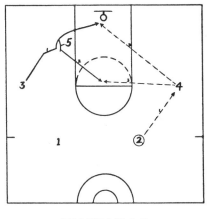

DIAGRAM 2-9
Split-In-and-Out

With this series of slashes combined with fakes, combined with quick moves to the side of the ball or to the opposite side, there is internal movement forcing the defense back while also setting the next step, which is the balance wheel.

3. The Balance Wheel

The balance wheel is just a way of describing an offense following the process of scrambling up players when movements of the initial Cut-and-Slash do not work. In other words, after the first two movements, often there is a mass of unorganized players grouped around the basket. The balance wheel fills a void to continue the offensive effort.

I have often marveled at the success of this part of the attack. The concept is to balance the floor as quickly as possible while looking for a pass, a move, or a shot. The other alternative is to pass the ball around horn (perimeter of the wheel) for a move or jump shot. This balance wheel is really the formation of a perimeter attack. A perimeter attack exists when players station themselves in various areas in a half-circle approximately ten to 21 feet from the basket ready to pass or to receive a pass for a shot or move. The balance wheel was developed after I observed the devastating effects of collapsing defenses against inside scorers. These tactics crippled offensive players inside with no available shot. Big centers often felt the sting of the collapsing defenses.

When the ball is passed out to start the attack, each player has the chance to do these things:

1. Drive in for a lay-up.
2. Drive, stop and jump shoot.
3. Jump shoot.
4. Pass to an open man on the perimeter.

This is an individual fundamental attack, permitting players to free-lance.

The floor spots for setting up the wheel are outlined in Diagram 2-10. The attack is set up as close to the basket as the defense allows.

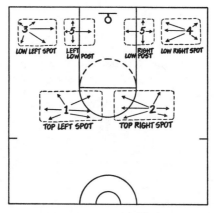

DIAGRAM 2-10
Balance Wheel Floor Spots

In the diagram the arrows show the potential movements as well as listing the names of the spots. They are: the low right spot, the top right spot, the top left spot, the low left spot, and the low post spot. The wheel is built initially on the side of the ball. Then players fill in the other spots in sequence relative to ball position. Diagram 2-11 shows a typical balance wheel alignment. Four passes the ball out to 2 in a low right spot. One moves to fill in the top right spot, 3 moves to the top left spot, 4 moves to fill in the lower left spot, while 5 moves to the left low post position. Four and 5 may reverse or screen for each other to confuse the defense. The wheel develops as the ball is passed around the perimeter. Often this delaying tactic catches a slow-reacting defense unable to defend against a quick jump shot. Diagram 2-12 shows

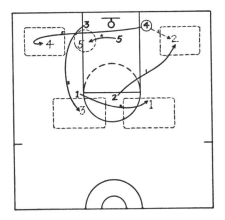

DIAGRAM 2-11
Typical Balance Wheel Alignment

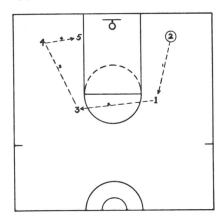

DIAGRAM 2-12
Perimeter Passing and Hitting the Low Post Player

the passes around the perimeter. Any player may free-lance or the ball may be moved to the weak side in preparation for the fourth step, the weak-side slash.

The value of the balance wheel is borne out by the fact that it is possible to use the attack against any defense—and particularly any time the offense breaks down.

4. The Weak-Side Slash

The weak-side slash follows the balance wheel after the player receiving the ball moves the ball around the wheel to the opposite area of the play origin. From this point one of several things can happen. The player on the weak side can make an individual drive; he can use any variety of two-man plays; he can give and go with the center; he can shoot; or he can pass the ball underneath to the low post man. A weak-side slash opens up avenues of scoring, of using individual capabilities, and of movement to the basket.

The value of this attack is derived from two sources. First, when the ball is passed away from the origin of the balance wheel, the defense must make adjustments to compensate for each pass. This adjustment may not be made, quickly creating defensive problems. The probing tactics presented by the balance wheel force more adjustments. Thus the defensive players are vulnerable. The second purpose is to develop a slashing attack while the defense is vulnerable making the adjustments. The slashes gear for inside-out scoring, too. The slashes include scoring off screen plays, clear-outs, and sharp passes to a low post man.

Six slashing plays will be explained along with the offensive options in Chapters 7 through 11. However, two examples are shown in Diagrams 2-12 and 2-13. In Diagram 2-12 the ball is passed around

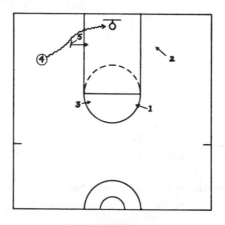

DIAGRAM 2-13
Weak-Side Slash

the balance wheel from 2 to 1 to 3 to 4, who passes it into the low post man, 5. Five can shoot or play one-on-one against his defensive man. In Diagram 2-13, with the ball already in 4's possession, 4 dribbles off a screen set up by 5. He dribbles to the basket while 5 rolls in for a pass or to rebound. The dribbler, 4, could also go to the right of 5.

If the weak-side slash is unsuccessful, then the balance wheel can be formed again and a weak-side slash can take place again. This time the ball would not necessarily have to be passed around the perimeter to start the attack but rather could start on either side.

IMPLEMENTATION OF THE FOUR STEPS IN THE CUT-AND-SLASH

It is necessary to spell out the occasions when the four steps in the Cut-and-Slash can be used effectively. There are defenses where only some of the steps should be utilized because of the prevailing defense's alignments and maneuvers. The following presents a sequence of the four steps in the offense against the various defenses:

Defense	*Offense*	*Steps*
Man-for-man	Six option patterns	Cut Slash Balance wheel Weak-side slash
Zones	Zone clocking pattern	Cut Balance wheel
Man-for-man full-court pressure	Six option patterns	Cut Slash Balance wheel Weak-side slash
Zone full-court pressure	Six option patterns	Cut Balance wheel
Half-court man-for-man pressure	Six option patterns	Cut Slash Balance wheel Weak-side slash
Half-court zone pressure	Zone patterns	Cuts Balance wheel
Combination (all)	Six option patterns or Zone clocking patterns	Cuts Balance wheel Weak-side slashes

A study of the four different steps will show that with these movements there are many scoring possibilities along with excellent movements into rebounding positions. The balanced floor positioning takes place, and there are always players in defensive set positions. Players are in position and ready to move back on defense for protection. Three players can go to the boards and there always is at least one man back and another man in position to get back for defensive positioning.

COACHING GUIDELINES

1. Passes to start the cuts should be crisp and originate from a guard to a forward or from a guard to a center.
2. Players should vary fakes and change pace to free themselves.
3. Return passes should be sharp, crisp, and either the overhead, chest, or bounce pass.
4. The cutter should always be alert to receive a pass while in the shooting area.
5. The cutter can use various individual movements before moving out of the internal area to set a screen for the slasher. The slasher can go either way around a screen.
6. If the defense switches, the dribbler should look for the screener to be clear.
7. The balance wheel should be formed with players filling in the five wheel positions with quick movement which may also be preceded with fakes.
8. If no play is available upon receiving a pass in the balance wheel, then the player receiving the pass must keep the ball moving around the perimeter to another clear man.
9. Often a pass may be made out from inside the three-second zone by a pivot man who may be covered. Consequently, the balance wheel may be very tight and allow for eight- to ten-foot jump shots.
10. The weak-side slash immediately follows the balance wheel, and may often be started with a pass to the pivot man or with a sudden explosive drive.
11. If the weak-side slash is unsuccessful, the ball may be passed around the perimeter to another player to initiate the weak-side slash again.

3

Attack Options
of the Cut-and-Slash

The Cut-and-Slash offense is comprised of six basic options. The object of all six individual options is to open the door for scoring from anywhere on the court or from any lane. Each option has its own vital characteristic which leads to opportunities for shooting and scoring. All of the options begin with a cut, then include the other steps when necessary. The cuts are different in each option, as are the slashes. But the balance wheel is utilized identically in each option, while the weak-side slash is composed of six different slashes, and any of the six may be used in all six options. The number of steps to be used vary with the opponents' defense, as was emphasized in Chapter 2.

Another key factor is that each attack option originates with a pass rather than a dribble. The pass may be made from guard to forward or guard to center. This pass keys the option and attack area. However, the steps may involve different players. For example, the guards may be involved in an option but may not participate in another except to make the initial pass starting the option.

Along with the six options to be discussed are the basic individual offensive fundamentals which are very pertinent to the option or movement. These fundamentals are vital to the attack because without the six offenses the attack would be ineffective, and without the basic necessary fundamentals the attack would be equally ineffective.

Basically, most teams include in their repertoire of offensive plays methods of driving, along with various types of shots. Practical footwork and sharp movements free players with or without the ball to score. The skills demand essential offensive basic expertise that goes beyond the general fundamentals taught in most other systems. These skills tend to render the individual—and consequently the offense —more potent.

There will perhaps be a tendency to think that six options may be too much to teach a team. I have found this untrue, because longitudinal trends in basketball indicate unmistakably that ball players are aspiring to ever higher levels of learning. Players are much smarter and can utilize more moves, shots and drives today than they could two decades ago. In my own coaching experience, I have found that teams I coached 15 years ago were not too different in potential raw ability than teams I observe now, but because of lack of coaching expertise, and perhaps lack of an understanding of aspirations and goals, the boys in that era did not have the opportunity to learn as much about the game of basketball or did not receive the skills training that the modern player is exposed to. Teams do a lot more on the court today than coaches dreamed possible 15 or 20 years ago.

There are drills and teaching methods to speed up the learning and performing process. These will be discussed thoroughly in the chapter on drills.

THE SIX BASIC OPTIONS

The six options to be discussed can be used in various ways. A team may elect to use only two or three options in a particular ball game; in other cases a team may use each option at one time or another during the contest; while in still other situations an option may be used along with deceptive pressing tactics and with the standard zone attack. Generally speaking, players should look for defensive weaknesses and then utilize the option or options designed to exploit the disadvantages of the defense. The order of using options may also vary. Sometimes teams use an option for several minutes, then go to another one—only to return to the original offense later on. Each game is treated on an individual basis and according to the immediate situation.

1. The X Attack

Usually against a man-for-man defense, start with an X Attack.

The key reason for this is to use two cutters and to create an opportunity for the forwards to move away from the basket. This option with the two cutters helps identify lazy guards and also promotes a chance to test the movements of their big men on defense. Look to see if they are reluctant to move away from the basket area and also to see if they can guard out-court. Players possessing weak defensive fundamentals stand out in this type of defensive maneuver. Players who are loafing can be taken advantage of right away. Another point is that if the opposition has a weak rebounding small player, the offense takes him under the offensive boards and exploits this weakness. One final point is that if an opponent likes to fast-break, then the small men are out of position to act as outlet men while the big men are away from rebounding position near the boards. Since there is a continual flow of fast-action movement, we seek to acclimate the team to involvement and movement.

Beginning the game with the X Attack also gives the potential of attacking any type of defense. This is true against full-court pressure, and specifically against the man-for-man type of pressure. Defensive players are moved away from the basket while we are racing in to score, giving us a definite advantage.

2. The Center-Out Attack

The Center-Out Attack is used in almost every contest and has great value in that it gives good-shooting pivot men an opportunity to move into the corner for a shot. This works well against defensive centers who refuse to move away from the basket to protect the corners. It also pulls big centers away from the near-basket area to protect against the pivot man on a hot-shooting night. It is a smooth-flowing offense with both inside and outside shooting opportunities made available with a minimum of effort.

3. The Rub-Off Offense

The Rub-Off Offense is used predominantly against man-for-man defenses and has extensive value in movement of the defense, potential lay-up shots by two cutters, and for springing loose the pivot man for a quick move-in play and lay-up shot. One more facet is that it can be used as a change-of-pace offense during certain parts of a game whenever players fall into a pattern of standing still or of being reluctant to move as a team.

4. The Weak-Side Attack

The versatile Weak-Side Attack is used in almost every game. It can be used to attack the opposite side of the court in respect to location of the ball, and it offers a sequence of moves for close-in shots from strategic areas. Although my teams do make cross-court passes, it is fundamentally sound to use two passes to attack the weak-side areas. These are rendered very accessible by the Weak-Side Crash Attack. This attack offers excellent maneuvers against pressure defenses, and it is very basic in its ability to move the ball to the basket efficiently as well as to provide lay-ups at the end of the charge. One can take advantage of poor weak-side defensive play with this option.

5. The 3-on-3 Attack

The 3-on-3 Attack is a power attack utilizing the versatility of big men against tall, immobile opponents. It is very possible to secure good shots close to the basket. It is more effective against half-court man-for-man defenses, and it is used in almost every game. The big players move often and also remain in close proximity to the basket for rebounding.

6. The Replacement Attack

The Replacement Attack is prevalent in every game. It offers a chance to combat full-court pressure quickly and efficiently, as well as to open scoring avenues in close to the basket, with the specific movements. The essentials of the option establish movement along a side lane until reaching a scoring area. Then the ball can be passed to the basket for good shots in the internal high percentage scoring zone.

IMPORTANT BASIC OFFENSIVE FUNDAMENTALS

There are important basic fundamentals that are a little different from the common fundamentals used in most attacks by other teams. These fundamentals must be mastered in order to properly develop the Cut-and-Slash Attack. Since this attack is characterized by many opportunities for close-in shooting and close-in movements, the individuals must develop versatility in that area. This versatility must be learned by each player, and it must be used effectively. Players must learn how to play with or without the ball in developing the attack.

A player must develop moves to get clear and to dominate the defensive man whenever his team gains ball possession. This must be accomplished anywhere on the court and particularly in the internal zone area. Granted, it takes movement to get into this area, but once a player gains ball possession here, he must be versatile enough to develop a shooting opportunity. Off-the-ball movements spring potential shooters loose and are essential for that reason.

Body Balance

The latest theory in all aspects of any sport emphasis is that the athlete must perform with precise timing, rhythm and physical smoothness. Coaches have discovered and stressed the fact that great athletes possess the three basics of timing, rhythm, and smoothness in every sport in the world. Basketball is an excellent example of this type of thinking. The slow-motion cameras being used now bring out the analytical accuracy of these fundamentals. Film of the great professional players discloses the finesse with which these giant men move. The fundamentals to be described involve the timing, rhythm, and smoothness in the development and use of body movements in basketball.

These body movements can only be realized if the player has control over his body. In other words, body control is the chief essential to be learned if the player is to be outstanding. Body control evolves from the regular basketball stance position. In the stationary position the player stands with his upper body over the balls of his feet with knees slightly flexed, back bent slightly, and head up; the player is relaxed but ready to move.

In the moving position the body should be bent at the waist with the upper torso slightly ahead of the hips.

The player should avoid standing or running in an upright position, nor should there be excessive leaning in any single direction. The legs should remain under the shoulders except when they stretch out to take steps. In running, the player should keep everything still except his legs and arms, and not attempt to run so fast that the natural smoothness of body coordination is lost; this can disturb the body balance. There should be a cruising speed with maximum coordination between legs and arms. Any other types of movements should be conducive to and in keeping with smooth coordination between his legs and the rest of his body.

The player must have his body under control to run, change directions, and stop at any time. Sudden changes in movement occur in fractions of seconds and can only be made if the player has complete body control. Versatility can only be acquired if body control and body balance have been developed.

Footwork

In order for a player to learn body control, he must master basic footwork. Basic types of movements can make a player much more effective but can only be acquired through a high degree of development of footwork necessary for basketball movement. It is better, in my estimation, to stereotype the various footwork movements in basketball—particularly in offensive play, and especially in close to the basket. The opposite extreme of just allowing a player to use any type of footwork leads to many fundamental mistakes. One important movement is pivoting. There are certain pivots that are much more effective than others while in close to the basket. Players learning footwork and pivoting patterns can use their basic offensive moves to a very high degree of efficiency. Generally, footwork involves quick starts, sudden stops, change of directions, change of pace, pivot, or a combination of several of these.

Stopping

The one footwork fundamental I found in need of development for outstanding offensive technique is stopping. A player capable of braking to a sudden stop with or without the ball is potentially very sound and a real offensive threat. A small player with stopping ability while dribbling can often attack a bigger opponent or a center with ease while getting off a shot in that closely guarded area. Stopping allows for the quick jump shot over taller opponents. Stopping is a key to offensive prowess and a must for each player—but particulary for the shorter players. Quick starts and sudden stops are a great combination for a player to develop. I can think of four excellent small players who possessed this combination and were all instrumental in championship teams. They were James Coleman, 5'6", and Billy Harper, 5'7", both from Eastern High School, and Billy Hassett, 5'8", and Guy DeLaire,

5'6", both from Windsor University. These four players were masters at starting and stopping and used this ability to upset many of their opponents with these tactics. Stopping is an absolutely vital offensive ingredient.

The Inside Pivot

There are two times when a player must consider offensive footwork. One is when he has the ball in his possession, and the other is when he moves to receive a pass. If a player has the ball in his possession and dribbles in close to the basket, he can use practically any type of footwork, with the only stipulation being that he spread his feet apart to allow for a wider base and better balance.

If a player moves in to receive a pass in the three-second area, then, upon catching the ball, he should come to a jump stop or a one-two stop with the inside foot established as the pivot foot. From that position, he can do many things. For example, if he enters that zone from the left side, he can drive right, cut back to the left, fake and drive, reverse pivot, drive, or jump shoot. A hook shot or a flip shot is also possible.

In Diagram 3-1, player 2 passes the ball to player 3 in the three-second lane. Three has come to a parallel jump stop, as noted by his feet, so he can effectively move or shoot as described. The inside or left foot becomes the pivot foot.

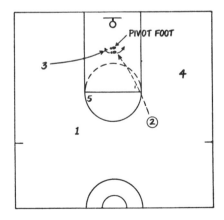

DIAGRAM 3-1
Establishing the Inside Pivot Foot

The importance of the inside pivot foot must again be stressed, since the burden of the attack and scoring takes place in close to the basket and establishes a great need for a wide assortment of moves and shots. Without mastery of these fundamentals, close-in scoring loses its effectiveness. Emphasis must also be placed upon the dribbler entering the three-second lane to use the inside foot to pivot in case of roll-back moves, and also in case the dribbler stops dribbling and shoots or fakes and shoots.

Movements Without the Ball

Some of the basic movements necessary either to free oneself to receive a pass or to free a player with the ball are used by players from each position. Some of these off-the-ball moves have been used for a long time in the game of basketball. They can be given a new twist, or they can be used standardly as in the past. Moving without the ball involves stops, changes of direction, changes of pace, or a combination of all three—which of course emphasizes the necessity of sound footwork. In the off-the-ball movement, the main concern is the type of movement itself rather than the footwork, which is rather basic in this case. The next series of diagrams shows the different important player movements without the ball.

Diagram 3-2 shows the simple *flat-cut*. The writer likes to use the term "flat-cut" as opposed to straight-cut, direct-cut or wing-cut,

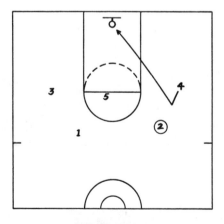

DIAGRAM 3-2
Simple Flat-Cut

primarily because he learned the term a long time ago from Coach Joel Mason, formerly the head coach at Wayne State University in Detroit. Coach Mason served as consultant to many coaches in our area. He used basketball terms which were simple and concise and consequently many of us learned and adopted his basketball vocabulary for use in our own systems. In the diagram, 4 moves toward 2 (who has the ball), suddenly stops abruptly on his left foot, then breaks for the basket. He can receive a pass from 2 or just clear out the area for 2 to drive.

The *forward exchange move* is used to clear a forward for an offensive opportunity, or to force the defensive men closer to the basket and allow the offense to start with less opposition in its proper alignment. This is used often against defensive players overplaying aggressively. This exchange is described in Diagram 3-3. Three and 4 move toward the baseline simultaneously, make a stop, move one or

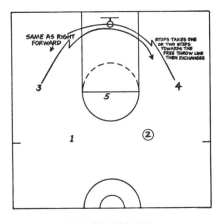

DIAGRAM 3-3
Forward's Exchange Move

two steps back toward mid-court, then with three quick steps proceed to exchange positions with 4 on the right always going to the baseline side and 3 to the free-throw line side to avoid confusion and an unnecessary collision. In other words, the man on the right is nearest to the baseline. These tactics serve to run the defensive players into a hook-up situation.

Diagram 3-4 shows the *clear and screen move*. It is standard

DIAGRAM 3-4
Clear-Out and Screen for Opposite Forward

procedure for a forward to do one of two things when a ball handler dribbles at him. He can screen-and-roll or he can clear out. When he clears out, the final part of his movement involves a screen for the other forward to either get clear for a pass or serve as a rebounder.

In the illustration, 2 dribbles at 4 and to the basket. Four clears out to the left side and screens for 3. Three then moves into rebounding position. Four moves into the role of defensive man, while 5 becomes a rebounder. One also stays back for defensive purposes. Often it is possible to get the tip-in on the shot attempt when 3 gets a clear rebound attempt of a missed shot, since his man often is picked off by 4's screen.

The *fake clear-out and screen* is shown in the next diagram, 3-5.

DIAGRAM 3-5
Fake Forward Clear-Out and Screen

Four starts to clear, then returns with a sharp movement to set a pick at the foul line extended at the circle to allow 2 to drive off him toward the basket. Four then rolls to the basket for a pass or rebound. The other players are rebounders or defensive players.

The *guard clear-out* works on the same assumption. The player without the ball either picks or clears out. In Diagram 3-6, 2 dribbles toward 1, who clears out, then 2 can pass off or work with 3. This move is designed for guards who overplay 1 and allows for the passing lane in the back court to open up.

Moves by the center without the ball quite often end up in easy shots or at least allow the pivot man to get the position he desires in the pivot. The *center-up-and-go move* is shown in Diagram 3-7. Two has

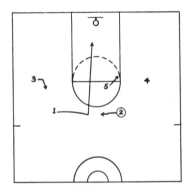

DIAGRAM 3-6
Guard Clear-Out

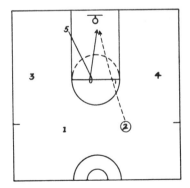

DIAGRAM 3-7
Center-Up-and-Go Move

the ball, 5 moves toward the foul line, then makes a pivot moving between his defensive man and the basket and holds the man off for a fraction of a second, then moves to the basket. As simple as this play may be, it still works very effectively each game against man-for-man defenses. The secret is for the post man to keep working at getting loose the whole game and, with two or three definite movements, to fake before positioning to pivot.

There are two forward and guard movements that are vital. The first one is the *simple reverse*. This is an exchange between the guard and the forward on the weak side. The move is designed to keep the defense honest or to set up a jump shot just beyond the foul line. Diagram 3-8 depicts this play. Two has the ball, while 1 moves to the

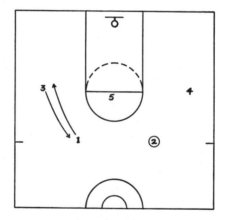

DIAGRAM 3-8
Simple Guard and Forward Reverse

inside of 3, who moves to the outside of 1. They simply exchange positions. This can also be effective for a shot against zones. Now with the two players in the new positions, the *reverse-and-screen* is the second guard and forward movement. The object is to have a screen set by the forward to allow the guard an opportunity to move to the boards in case of a shot. It also frees the forward for a short jumper just outside the free-throw line on a switch by the defense. Diagram 3-9 shows 2 passing the ball to 4 to start a play. One screens for 3, who moves outside of 1 to the basket for a rebound or return to his normal position. One can shoot from the short outside position.

The *guard reverse* is a simple exchange by the guards to once again keep the man-for-man defense honest and to keep the passing

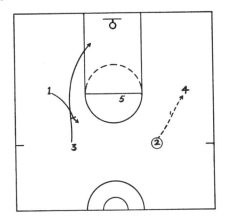

DIAGRAM 3-9
Guard and Forward Reverse-and-Screen

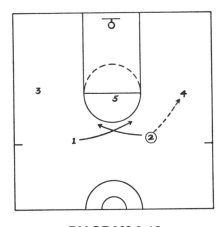

DIAGRAM 3-10
Guard Reverse

lanes open between forwards and guards. The man passing the ball this time exchanges to the inside while the other guard stays on the outside. In Diagram 3-10, 2 passes to 4 and exchanges positions with 1 by moving inside or closer to the basket, while 1 passes outside or closer to mid-court.

Movements with the Ball

Movements with the ball are geared to make the players more effective by driving to the basket with the ball. Players able to take the ball to the basket for a shot put a lot of pressure on the defensive team.

This is especially true if all players show adeptness at these skills. Players in my experience have done a fine job at this task, and many games were won because of these competencies.

Since I concentrate on giving the big men scoring opportunities on the pattern offense, it is necessary for them to master movements with the ball on an individual basis. These movements generally take place prior to the formal initiation of the pattern or during each step whenever a player is in a one-on-one situation.

Four individual moves comprise the *roll-back series*, which can be used by all players in a one-on-one play—but particularly by the guards and forwards.

The first move to be learned is the *across-and-down*. This is accomplished by the forward dribbling, with the hand away from the defensive man, to the foul-line area, and then with a pivot and roll dribble driving to the basket for a lay-up or close-in shot. In Diagram 3-11, 3 has the ball and dribbles to the free-throw area and rolls to the

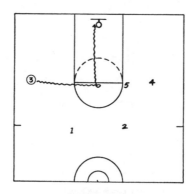

DIAGRAM 3-11
Across-and-Down

basket after the pivot. This rolling type of move is an excellent move to get free with the ball. A key is to teach the forward to drive past the middle of the court in the free-throw line area. Then he can make the direct line to the basket. This forces the defensive man under the basket and into a poor situation to block the shot, and offers the dribbler an easy lay-up shot.

The sister move to the across-and-down is the *down-and-up*. This move is opposite to the other. In other words, the forward dribbles to the baseline, then reverses and comes up to the front of the basket for a lay-up or hook shot. Again, it is important to dribble all the way to the baseline in order to allow for the roll-back to end up in close to the basket.

In Diagram 3-12, 3 has the ball and dribbles to the left baseline, pivots and rolls back to the top or front of the basket into position for a shot.

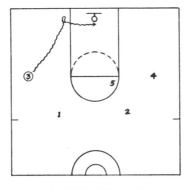

·DIAGRAM 3-12
Down-and-Up

Another related roll-back type of move is the *stutter-and-in*. The object of this move is to start driving to the basket (either the forward or guard can do this), fake a rollback with a big step and delay, then drive in hard to the basket. This has been a blue chip move for my teams for years. Diagram 3-13 shows 3 with the ball. He drives toward the basket, fakes a roll-back move, then with a burst of speed drives to the basket.

There is one more move in the roll-back series. This move is the *dribble-in-and-back,* which is performed with a guard (or forward, at times) driving in to the basket and entering the three-second lane. He then backs up with the dribble while still facing the basket and either passes to a post man, drives in again for the lay-up, or jump shoots. This play is extremely vital in developing an effective individual attack, and it has served well through the years. I first saw and identified it as a move when Clarence Straughn, the fine guard on Wayne State's team in the middle 50's, used it so effectively against all opponents. He would drive hard for the basket, then dribble back and pinpoint

DIAGRAM 3-13
Stutter-and-In

excellent passes to the pivot man or drive in for an easy shot, or hit with his excellent outside shot. Dave Bing, the superstar guard of the Detroit Pistons, used this move often in piling up his points and assists.

The move is depicted in Diagram 3-14. One has the ball and starts a drive, while 3 clears out. One then moves in for an attempted shot. If this is not possible, he backs up and if the defensive man follows him, he darts for the basket. He can also pass or jump shoot.

Passing Off to Baseline Man

Now that ways of moving to get free have been explained, along with ways of moving to the basket with the ball, it is necessary to indicate the importance of being able to pass to the baseline man. This player could be the pivot man or any other player on the baseline. The two-on-one under the basket is an extremely vital play in the whole offense, because with the cutting and slashing movements we often break loose a lay-up-bound dribbler who is apprehended by the defensive pivot man or the man guarding the baseline man. This means that the dribbler must make a decision either to go for the basket or to pass off to the baseline man. The important thing is to have body control, ball control, and be perceptive before making a decision as to the choice of attack. There is no rush to make a decision, and the longer a ball handler can wait, the better off he is and the more chance he has to complete the play and convert it into a score. Waiting denotes a fraction of a second.

DIAGRAM 3-14
Dribble-In-and-Back

There is an old cliché in basketball that goes something like "You do this and I'll do that." The meaning is to do the opposite of what the defensive man does. In this case, if the defensive man drops back, then shoot; if he challenges, then pass off; if he jumps up to block the shot, shoot if it is possible or else pass off to the open man. This dynamic internal zone play can rip even the best defenses to shreds if handled properly.

Diagram 3-15 shows the mechanics of this fine play in the internal zone. One has the ball and dribbles for the basket. When 5's man tries

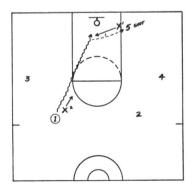

DIAGRAM 3-15
Two-on-One with the Baseline Man

to stop the drive, 1 passes off to 5 for the lay-up shot. This is simple but effective and available frequently in every game.

Combination Play

Finally, there is a combination play that works quite well. This is valuable because it involves a series of moves off the ball when the ball is possessed at the high post position. Normally one of the best ways for the post man to score is to drive directly to the basket one-on-one, or head fake down and shoot the jumper. There is also an excellent play opportunity for a pass and return pass and shot. In Diagram 3-16,

DIAGRAM 3-16
Combination Play

the ball is in 5's possession; meanwhile, 4 breaks to the basket for a pass, then moves out to screen for 3, who breaks across to the right side and close to the basket. Five passes to 3, fakes a break to the basket, then drops behind 3 for a return pass and a short jump shot. This move is excellent against sagging man-for-man defenses.

All of the plays discussed here play a very distinct part in my teams' offense and must be learned and utilized to make their style of attack highly effective. A discussion of the options and fundamentals leads to understanding of both in type of plays and unique fundamentals. With this understanding, it is appropriate to elaborate on the principles involved in the Cut-and-Slash attack.

COACHING GUIDELINES

1. The six options generally compose the Cut-and-Slash offense development.
2. Options can be used in various ways to counteract the various defenses.
3. The key points of the options are the foundation of a versatile attack that makes the offense effective against any defense.
4. There are enough characteristics of the options to attack various defenses, and a team can use some or all of the options in each game.
5. A successful option should be used until defensive adjustments are made, then a switch should be made to another option to take advantage of defensive weaknesses that are created by the adjustments.
6. Individual movement fundamentals are the foundation of the implementation of the effective attack.
7. Considerations must be made for movements with or without the ball.
8. Timing, rhythm, and smoothness characterize the outstanding player.
9. Players moving into the pivot for a pass should use the inside pivot to be really effective, and to avoid unnecessary turnovers.
10. The object of cutting and slashing is to create close-in shooting with one-on-one and two-on-one situations.

4

Basic Principles
of the Cut-and-Slash

It is now time to deal with basic principles which will apply to the total Cut-and-Slash offense. An understanding of these principles will clarify and simplify the understanding of the offense. In applying these principles to the six options which will be discussed individually later on, it is found that the commonality of the principles can be success-fully used to make the options much more effective. It is necessary to organize the attack on the basis of these particular principles to allow for comprehension and a more articulate and integrated clarification of the options. In considering basic principles, the concern is for learning the key factors involved and the underlying thinking as to why and how progressive order against certain types of defense takes place. The use of basic principles against man-to-man defenses, against zone de-fenses, against full-court man-to-man pressure defenses, and against full-court zone pressure defenses must be installed properly for the attack to be cohesive.

Some of the considerations which may be effectively borne in mind when confronted with both man-to-man and zone defenses are: (1) to move as quickly as possible to the basket for the shot, (2) to have movement enough to get a man underneath for a shot, (3) to find an open man if there is no shot available off the first thrust, (4) to get into position and make adjustments for strong offensive rebounding, (5) to attack the internal zone, keeping in mind the "inside-out" scoring theory, (6) to use the court lane area attacking principle, (7) to use the fast-break front-court alignment against pressure defenses, (8) to exercise patience by waiting for the good shot rather than foolishly taking a bad shot, and (9) to keep the floor balanced for offensive purposes as well as defensive purposes.

This last point means that we want three men rebounding and two men in defensive positions. One player should be back beyond the 21-foot mark from the offensive basket and is considered strictly a defensive man, while the other player may remain somewhere in the area of the foul line and he too is a defensive man and also considered an offensive man. In other words, have one-and-a-half players on the defensive at all times for protection. One other fact should be related, and that is if nothing offensively is possible, even with all the movements, then the continuity phase is simply added to the offense by running through the option from the beginning again. Because many opportunities prevail along the way, the continuity part of the attack is seldom necessary.

PRINCIPLES IN ATTACKING MAN-TO-MAN DEFENSES

A major concern in attacking man-to-man defenses is knowing exactly where the defensive team contests the offensive attack. It is found that very few teams nowadays, even in high school, play a true drop-back type of defense. A drop-back defense is formed when a team gets back in a shell inside the 21-foot area of the basket. Most team defenses have a variation of three defensive men near the basket but will invariably pressure the ball with the two front men. When attacking the complete drop-back type of man-to-man defense, the composition of our attack is similar to the one used originating from around mid-court. The only difference, of course, is that there is less running room and less passing room, but it is easier to attack the drop-back defense and force opponents under the basket. If it isn't possible to go inside for a shot, then it is found to be very easy to set up shots just outside the perimeter of the defense.

In reviewing attacking all types of man-to-man defenses, assume that there is pressure by the defense on the two guards bringing the ball up.

I realize there are different philosophies in defensive play. For example, some dictate forcing the player with the ball away from the middle court area. Other concentrations are to overplay the next potential receiver. Then again there are different thoughts about the type of man-to-man defense to use. For example, some defenses use the sagging principle; others use the playing-tight principle; still others use a combination of both. The theory of starting the offensive play in either of the court lanes makes it possible to overpower these tactics and convert them into offensive advantages.

Ideally, the attack against man-to-man defenses can originate most effectively from an area near mid-court. The reason for this is the vulnerability of the defense due to the extensive area they must cover. There is considerable room to start the cutting prior to the follow-up slashing action. Once our players enter the front court against man-to-man defenses, and particularly with pressure on the players with the ball, our offense is ready to initiate the first thrust to the basket.

Ideal Starting Area

Diagram 4-1 depicts the area on a court most conducive for starting the offensive. The area ranges from mid-court to approximately ten

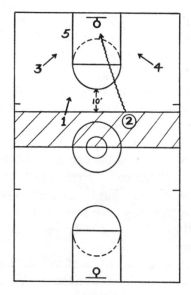

DIAGRAM 4-1
Ideal Offense Starting Area

feet from the top of the free-throw circle. In the diagram, player 2 drives toward the basket. If he gets by his man, of course he plays two-on-one against player 5's defensive man. This is an individual move, and it comes off what is called the *wave attack,* which will be discussed more thoroughly. The other players carry out an assignment too. For example, players 3 and 4 are rebounders and player 1 is a defensive man, while 5 plays two-on-one should he get by his man. A vital rule to inject here is that if a player holds the ball for more than three seconds, his teammates must exchange positions in order to have movement enabling him to pass to either one, or to dribble toward the basket. Diagram 4-2 shows the action in this type of play. Two has the

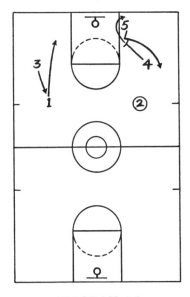

DIAGRAM 4-2
Exchange to Get Free to Receive a Pass

ball and cannot pass, so 1 and 3 exchange positions while 4 blocks for 5 and exchanges positions. Presumably someone will clear for a pass so 2 is able to move toward the basket.

The Wave Attack

In all outstanding offenses I feel that there must be an opportunity for individual play. A discipline offense is fine, but in true offensive attacking, a team must permit some individual movement if it is available prior to beginning the formal pattern. The *wave attack,* which is what I call the individual type of movements, is used sporadically just prior to starting any one of our six options against man-to-man or zones. As a rule, the option itself is usually begun unless the defense makes a mistake and allows the offense to take advantage with an individual maneuver for the shot. The wave attack has some weaknesses and, of course, the primary one is that the players may impatiently take advantage of the freedom opportunity and force movements which should not be made.

Some examples of the wave attack are depicted in Diagram 4-3. In this diagram, 2 has the ball, 1 reverses with 3 who comes to the foul

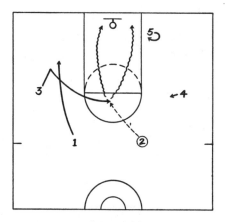

DIAGRAM 4-3
Wave Attack Individual Moves from the Free-Throw Line

line to receive a pass from 2 and has the option of driving to the basket either right or left. Four can be a defensive man or a rebounder, while 5 is an offensive man or a rebounder—to include floor balance in the attack. Another individual move off the wave attack is depicted in Diagram 4-4. Two has the ball and 5 puts a reverse screen on 4's man, allowing 4 to fake right and break left off 5 toward the basket. Two passes the ball to 4 if he is clear or waits for 5 to roll clear and then passes to him. One and 3 follow through with their responsibilities as rebounder and defensive man.

In Diagram 4-5, 2 again has the ball, and he is involved in one of the basic rules of driving. The rule states that if a person on offense drives at a player, the player must do one of two things: he must either

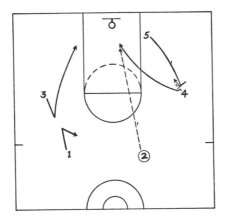

DIAGRAM 4-4
Wave Attack Reverse Screen

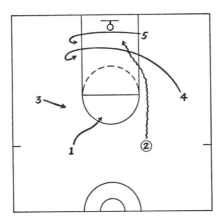

DIAGRAM 4-5
Wave Attack Forward and Center Clear-Out

screen for a pick-and-roll play or clear the area to allow 2 to drive. In this diagram, 2 drives to the basket while 4 and 5 clear to the opposite side of the court, giving 2 the opportunity to drive.

A final word about the wave attack is that upon receiving a pass, a player has the option of passing, shooting or driving, in accordance with his perception of the offensive possibilities.

Combating the Tight-Slide-Through Defense

The *tight-slide-through defense* is the easiest to attack successfully. The reason for this is that a man can be sprung loose with quick maneuvers or inside screen-and-roll plays. One of the five defensive men is vulnerable to these plays in this type of attack. This is especially true against bigger, slower players—particularly when we have any kind of continual movement at all.

Combating the Sag

The *sagging defense* creates more problems than any other type. In this defense, it is still possible to attack successfully, but it is more difficult to get easy crib shots. We can create situations with outside screening, forcing the defensive man toward the three-second area to enable players to take short jump shots. A roll-in is also available for a potential lay-up. Diagrams 4-6 and 4-7 show this attack. In Diagram 4-6, 2 has the ball and passes it to 4. He then runs straight to the basket

DIAGRAM 4-6
Outside Guard and Opposite Forward Screen

and starts moving up along the three-second lane toward the foul line. Three moves in to screen his defensive man, who has sagged towards the ball; 3 thus creates a screen and jump shot possibility for 2. In Diagram 4-7 the follow-up of the play is shown. The 4 man returns the pass to the 1 man moving towards the ball. The 1 man passes to 2 who is behind an outside screen set by 3. Two has the opportunity to jump shoot, drive or pass off to the 3 man rolling to the basket.

Another similar play which has been successful in beating the sagging defense is shown in Diagram 4-8. In this diagram, the action is between the forward and the center. Two has the ball and passes to 1, who fakes and comes to meet the ball. One in turn passes to 5 who has

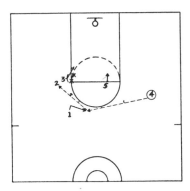

DIAGRAM 4-7
Outside Screen Shot or Roll-In

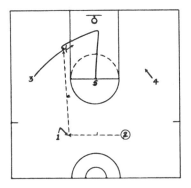

DIAGRAM 4-8
Forward and Center Outside Screen

moved form the foul line behind the screen set by 3 near the basket. After receiving the pass, 5 can either drive, shoot, or pass the ball to 3 moving towards the basket. These maneuvers can be implemented in the wave attack and are also vital; they can be integrated into the slashes and weak-side slashes in each option.

PRINCIPLES IN ATTACKING ZONE DEFENSES

I have utilized a unique method in attacking the zone defenses. Due to the enormous number of zone alignments and movements, standard rules have been designed to force the zone to move the way it must to invite an attack. There are usually only three ways zones align, regardless of the original type of zone. In other words, when the ball is in three different positions, all zones are in an approximately identical alignment. There is no significant disadvantage in various types of shifting movements on the part of the defensive players in assuming these alignment positions. However, by recognizing the defensive movements, the offense may gain an advantage in exploiting poor shifting.

The three positions are (1) with the ball left or right of the center court and just beyond the free-throw circle, (2) with the ball left or right of the foul line extended, and (3) with the ball in either the right or left corners. The zone shifts are identical. All zones mold into a defensive lineup with three players between the ball and the basket. The other two players are on either side of the three men or stand two in a row with the ball in the corner. The zone may be completely in the original alignment when the ball is located in the center post area. Consequently, by forcing the zone into one of the three alignments, the offense presumably has the advantage if it is prepared to attack out of these areas. In shifting to these defensive positions, the defense offers what we call passing lanes or passing avenues.

The lanes just discussed are shown in Diagrams 4-9, 4-10, and 4-11. In Diagram 4-9, 1 has the ball to the left of the circle, and in this position the defense will invariably be in the identical alignment with three men in line with the ball and one wingman on either side. The shaded areas depict the passing lane's potential. A passing lane may also mean that the player with the ball must pass it over the head of one player and be able to penetrate a lane deeply toward the basket. In Diagram 4-10, with the ball in side position at the foul line extended, four passing lanes, two inside lanes and two outside lanes are shown. Diagram 4-11, with the ball in the corner, illustrates the third alignment. There are three men in line with the ball and two up front. The passing lanes here are fewer, but there are still three areas in which to pass.

There is probably concern as to the possibilities of passing lanes when the ball is in the pivot area. Actually this is not an area that is used to open up the initial passing attack against zones. The post area definitely is used to beat the zones, but usually the intent is to force the zones into the recognized alignments and then take advantage of the potential passing lanes.

In attacking zone defenses, it is important that there be quick ball movement and also player movement. The movement of the players

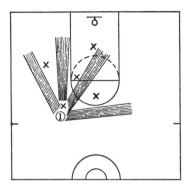

DIAGRAM 4-9
Zone Passing Lanes with Ball at Top Left Spot

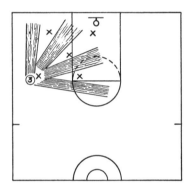

DIAGRAM 4-10
Zone Passing Lanes with Ball at Left Foul Line Extended Spot

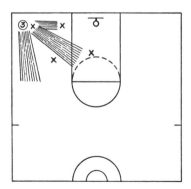

DIAGRAM 4-11
Zone Passing Lanes with Ball in Left Corner

naturally should involve getting into the open areas and being ready to shoot the ball upon receiving it, while other players move to rebounding position. Rebounding against zone defense is usually easier because many players get in the habit of standing around without blocking out in their zone areas.

Zone Wave Attack

Now that the possibilities of the passing lanes have been noted, Diagrams 4-12, 4-13, and 4-14 will show the potential player movements from the wave type of offense. Naturally in the chapter on offensive options the total option will be drawn out, but in order to understand these options more thoroughly, the principle of lanes and wave attack must be clearly stated.

In Diagram 4-12, the ball is secured by 1 at the top left position. Three is stationed in an open lane. Four moves into an open lane, 5 in another lane is the post man and 2 is in another lane. In this particular case, 4 receives a pass from 1 as the first choice. The second choice is

DIAGRAM 4-12
Zone Wave Attack from Top Left Spot

a pass to 3, the third possibility is a pass to 5, and the fourth possibility is a pass to 2. This order of passing indicates that we are offensive-minded, and the fourth pass is usually the outside pass that starts the pattern offense. In Diagram 4-13, the ball is at the left foul-line extended position, and players move into the open lanes. The ideal passing situation is shown by the number of the passes. Diagram 4-14

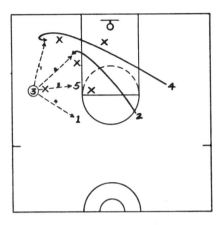

DIAGRAM 4-13
Zone Wave Attack from Left Foul Line Extended Spot

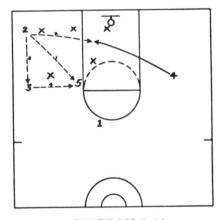

DIAGRAM 4-14
Zone Wave Attack from Left Corner

shows the possibilities with the ball in the left corner. Here again players try to move into open lane positions for shots, and the ideal passes are numbered. The number of the pass indicates the most suitable receiver and shooter. There is one variation: 2 passes to 3, who in turn passes to 5 in the pivot area—which is still a good play. One final comment about attacking zones is that the players should be alert to move into the passing lanes and keep the floor spread and stay in shooting position. They should receive the ball in position to take the quick jump shot. This is important to a successful attack.

The wave attack may be started by dribbling or passing the ball to one of these three locations. If nothing happens, then the regular zone offense is ready to begin. We have often sustained the wave attack for long periods of time without using any formal pattern.

Regular Zone Offense

The zone attack in this system was developed with three thoughts in mind. First, the offense should be applicable against all types of defenses; second, it should originate from any of the six options; and third, it should have player movements as well as ball movement. These three rules govern the regular attack. It has proven effective through the years. The attack begins with an option cut; then positions are taken as depicted in Diagram 4-15. Five assumes a post position on

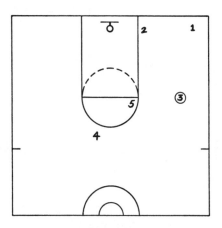

DIAGRAM 4-15
Regular Zone Offense Alignment

the side of the ball near the free-throw circle and free-throw area. Three has the ball at the free-throw line extended. One assumes a corner position. Four is located at the top of the circle to the left side, and 2 is at the right low post position.

Clocking Movements

This offense has the clocking type of movements which, while not new and original, are still useful and highly effective with some additional variations.

Diagrams 4-16, 4-17, and 4-18 show the three basic movements of clocking.

The initial clocking movement is shown in Diagram 4-16. Two passes the ball to 4 and goes away from his pass. He delays at the top of the circle for a possible weak-side play. Four dribbles away from the corner—but in a shooting area. Three moves clockwise to the corner for a possible shot or pass and dribbles out. One has moved to the right low post position, while 5 stands still at the high post position. The play may continue with a pass to 3, and he would dribble out as did 4, with the other players clocking to new positions.

The guard-to-weak-side play is shown in Diagram 4-17. Player 3 passes to player 4, who fakes left first, then moves to receive a pass.

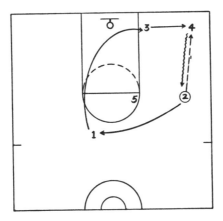

DIAGRAM 4-16
Initial Clocking Movement with Ball on Right Side

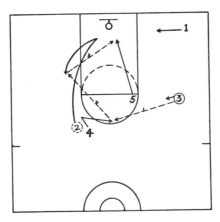

DIAGRAM 4-17
Guard-to-Weak-Side Play

Two moves toward the three-second lane en route to the right low post position, then stops abruptly and moves out for a pass from 4. Two can jump shoot or pass off to 5, who is moving to the basket. One would rebound.

The pivot weak-side is depicted in Diagram 4-18. The ball is passed from 3 to post man 5. Five passes to 4 on the short left side. He can shoot or drive. Five could cut to the basket for a return pass. Five could also pass to 2 or 1 if they are open.

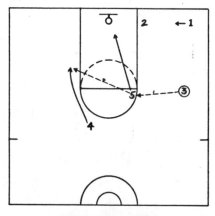

DIAGRAM 4-18
Center to Weak-Side

ATTACK COMBINATION DEFENSES

Actually we have used the regular offense (zone) to attack combination defenses. Combination defense is either a man-for-man defense with zone principles included, or a zone defense with man-for-man principles. The clocking movements open avenues necessary to combat this defense and its variations.

The movements would be reversed to counterclockwise if the attack started on the left side. The players would seek the opposite positions with movement going from left to right. The attack could start on one side of the court, then from a balance wheel could move to the opposite side and reverse the movements.

The Fast-Break Front-Court Alignment

In order to score consistently off the fast break, the man-for-man pressure offense, and the zone pressure offense, it is imperative to be highly organized in the front court. This is referred to as the fast-break front-court alignment, and is characterized by two tandems or triangles. These two tandems are the open and the closed tandems. With these two alignments, a team may converge on a basket outnumbering the defense, or by outmaneuvering the defense. The first choice is to attack two-on-one or three-on-two while forming the closed tandem. The second choice is to attack with a three-on-three or four-on-three from an open tandem. Both attacks end up with two wing men, a trailer, and a player at the free-throw line area who cuts to the basket, becoming another front man. The fifth man stays back as a safety man.

Closed Tandem

Diagram 4-19 shows the closed tandem with a trailer play. One is at the free-throw line, 2 is the right wing man, 3 is the left wing man,

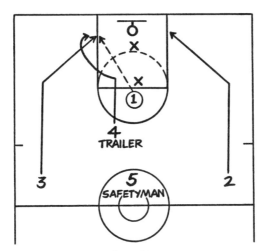

DIAGRAM 4-19
Closed Tandem with Pass to Left Wing Man

and 4 is the trailer, while 5 stays back. Here 4 is shown breaking to an outside wing position and is the third man up front. Diagram 4-20 shows a pass to the trailer, 4, who can shoot or pass the ball off to 3 if the defensive man tries to stop the short. This may become a screen-and-roll play.

Open Tandem

Diagram 4-21 shows the open tandem with 1 at the free-throw line possessing the ball. Three goes wide to the left wing position, 2 is at

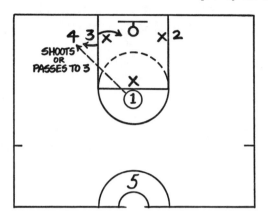

DIAGRAM 4-20
Closed Tandem Trailer

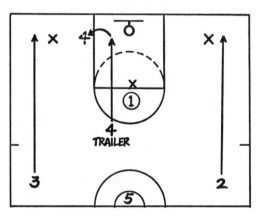

DIAGRAM 4-21
Open Tandem Alignment

the right wing position, and 4 is the trailer moving to the inside trailer position. Five is the safety man. This alignment offers the wing man a shot if the defense collapses on the trailer, and the trailer a shot if the wing men are covered. Four goes to a low post position if he doesn't receive a pass.

Diagram 4-22 shows a wing man to trailer play. One passes to wing man 3 who passes to trailer 4 under the basket for the shot.

There are many other ways to set up the tandem, but one favorite method merits mention. This is the first wing man to the corner. In Diagram 4-23, 1 has the ball at the free-throw area. Two is the first wing man on the right. He crosses over to the left corner. Three moves to the left wing position. Four assumes the right wing position. Usually 4 is clear for a lay-up if the defensive man follows 2. Two is clear if not

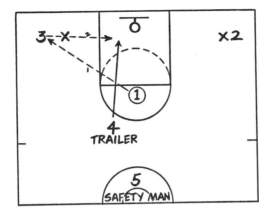

DIAGRAM 4-22
Open Tandem Wing Man to Trailer

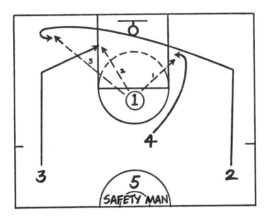

DIAGRAM 4-23
First Wing Man to Opposite Corner

followed for a corner shot. This is a combination of the closed and open tandems.

The start and development of the fast break is quite conventional and needs no further discussion, but the completion was developed because of the emphasis on the importance of the completion phase. Reference will be made to the front court organization, since this alignment was established in many of my offensive plays and particularly in thrusts against the pressure defenses.

Attacking Full Court Man-to-Man Pressure

The Cut-and-Slash reigns supreme against any type of full court pressure, including the full court man-to-man presses. The reason for this is that the organization with the options involved creates potentiality in scoring.

All six of the options involve utilizing player movement and ball movement to blend into a smooth and functional attack emanating into high percentage shot possibilities. The options are used on a basis of baseline-to-baseline attacking against pressure teams. The attack begins with similar movements as distinguished in each option. It then progresses into a fast-break front-court alignment. The exact attack will be diagrammed and spelled out in the chapters on the various options. The primary thought at this time is to consider the rules of order in challenging the man-for-man presses.

Traditionally inserted in many team offenses is a dribbling attack against the press, with the ball handler individually being responsible for bringing the ball through the clutching grasp of the press. Then he would start the official offensive pattern. This archaic type can still be useful, but it is not really practical. Too often the game becomes a dribbling contest with the offensive thrust terminating at the mid-court line while waiting for generation of the attack with the pattern. The offense should look for baseline-to-baseline scoring and start its pattern by inbounding the ball and putting the pattern into effect. Intention is lightning scoring a few seconds after the attack commences. There are no delay tactics, opening the door for the defensive pressure to force a breaking down of the attack or to force violations and turnovers. The pressure is applied to the defense instead, with the offense capitalizing on defensive mistakes. These mistakes may range from careless overplaying to individual loafing. With offensive pressure, the defense may become vulnerable and be rendered ineffective.

There are two basic thoughts in starting the offense. The first is to attack immediately after a basket or a delay on a turnover. The second is to allow a few seconds for teammates to assume the proper positions on the court. After this is accomplished, then the attack begins and the option used at the time becomes the pattern for attack. Both techniques are excellent, but they must be used properly or chaos will occur. In the former, the strategy is to beat the press before it can be established, while the latter tends to beat the press after it has been prepared for implementation.

The primary concern in the attack is to pass the ball inbounds, to move it up-court with organization, and to be organized to penetrate the basket for a good shot, with potential follow-up rebounding action.

The ball may be passed long for the quick attack or short for the deliberate attack.

Controlling the Attack

It is necessary to analyze the type of pressure defense the opponents install. Questions to resolve center around knowledge of the press mechanics. Is it an all-out press? Is it a passive press? Are they trapping? Do they attack continually? Do they drop back quickly? All of these are lead questions which must be answered for effective offensive attacking.

After acknowledging the type of press, it is possible to attack the press with adept precision, since the mechanics of the offense make allowances for the various tactics. One important factor to consider is that the floor must be divided into areas in order to keep a highly organized attack. Basically, divide the court up in terms of control areas and offensive areas for the simple reason that there are times when players must be in proper positions before attacking, and if there are strictly offensive areas, athletes will not be in the proper positions for the scoring thrust. Control areas mean even though the ball is moving up-court, the player with the ball is waiting to make sure his teammates are lining up ready for a thrust toward the basket. Once he gets into the offensive starting areas, the thrust begins.

Diagram 4-24 shows the method used to divide up the floor. Letter *A* is the first control area that is in the back court. *B* is the first attacking area, midway in the back court. *C* is the second controlling area, while *D* is the front court attacking area. It is pertinent to the attack that the principle of control areas and offense areas be adhered to in order to create a more potent offense.

Inbounding the Ball

Entering the ball against man pressure may be one of the most difficult parts of the whole attack. Against man-to-man, the six options can be used very successfully. The initial problem is to put the ball into play and have the men in the front court move enough to get free for a pass to start the offense. The individual or wave attack against full-court man-to-man is possible, too. The point in mind is dribbling the ball to the basket in zip-zap fashion and setting up a fast break align-

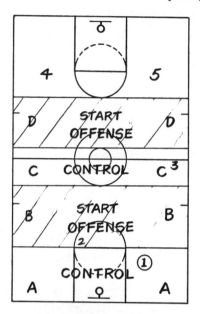

DIAGRAM 4-24
Floor Organization for Attacking Full-Court Pressure Defenses

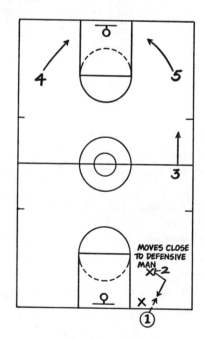

DIAGRAM 4-25
Davies Method to Get Clear for Pass Reception

ment. However, it is preferable to use one of the option attacks because of team coordination, which leads to many easy baskets.

Methods of throwing the ball in are varied, and the key is tied to the technique of individuals moving to get loose for a pass-in. This is extremely important. Diagram 4-25 shows the method of putting a ball into play. This is the individual method where a player moves two directions after a fake, and then moves to catch the inbounds pass. Years ago while attending the Adelphi Basketball Clinic in Long Island, New York, and during a night session with a group of fine, dedicated coaches, I spent time talking with Bob Davies, former professional player from the Rochester team. Bob had a theory that anybody could get loose for a pass. He outlined the procedure, stating that if a man wants a pass and is being pressured, he should move up tight against his opponent with his back to him. Then with a fake and one or two quick movements, go to the ball. His theory was that it is impossible for the defensive man to stay with an offensive man in that position who moves quickly. This fundamental worked extremely well for my team, which used it successfully for a long time. In Diagram 4-25, 2 uses the Davies method to get clear and receives a pass from 1.

Diagram 4-26 demonstrates the technique of freeing oneself for a pass-in from out of bounds. In this method an interchange between two

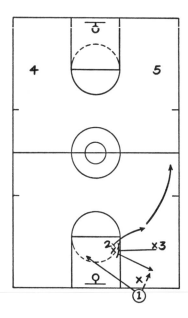

DIAGRAM 4-26
Screen Interchange to Get Free for Inbound Pass

players from a screen is used. Three screens for 2 by blocking out 2's defensive man, 2 breaks to the left of the screen, and 3 breaks back the opposite way for a pass. One of these two players should be unguarded and in position to receive a pass. Then 1 makes the pass. He can either follow the pass or go away from it, while if 3 catches the pass-in as in the diagram, then 2 will move upcourt to join 4 and 5, who are in position for an offensive attack.

Finally, against man-to-man pressure, if the player with the ball is trapped, he should pass the ball to an open man. This man in turn will bring the ball up to a spot in the offensive attack area. One of the options can be enforced from this point. These few principles are sufficient to guide the attack against a man-to-man type of full-court pressure.

PRINCIPLES IN ATTACKING FULL-COURT ZONE PRESSURE

Through the years the zone presses have had a significant impact on basketball. Ten years ago it was very difficult to successfully attack zone presses with the related intricacies to overcome these obstacles in order to win consistently. But in recent years offensive-minded coaches have been creative enough to develop theories of attack which can regularly overwhelm and defeat zone pressure defenses. Of course, there are certain general rules that have to be followed for success against such a defensive attack. Any carelessness by the offensive team can create troublesome situations, giving the pressure zone the advantage. In analyzing zone presses, it is found that there are many different alignments possible; still, ingenious coaches continue to design even more each year. In order to be successful against zone pressure, there has to be a method of reducing the effectiveness of such defenses with a simple but complete type of offensive attack.

My teams have extracted numerous ideas from other offensive theories in defeating the variations of zone presses, and they have reduced these ideas to the point of simplification for practical use. The general rules are: (1) Either attack quickly with long passes or take a few seconds to set up the option offense. (2) A player receiving a pass should be moving toward the ball. (3) A player who receives a pass should turn and look before moving up-court and be able to determine the location of the other nine players on the court. (4) A player shouldn't panic and lose his dribble. (5) A player should stay out of pinches or dangerous pinching areas. These are along sidelines and corners and the ten-second line. (6) If caught in a trap situation, a player should try to make any type of pass-out. Either a short pass or fake and pass may be used, but the player should get it out of the pinch. (7) A team should keep the floor balanced and players spread out. (8) A team should attack with the idea of going all the way in for a score. (9) A player should know whether the defensive team is trapping only in the back court or is trapping in the front court too. Also whether they retreat to the basic defense, after two trap attempts, or are trapping all over continually. (10) A player should know what drop-back basic defense opponents use. (11) A player should only dribble the ball to get away from a trap, or to take it to the basket. (12) When the defensive team has retreated inside the free-throw area, a player shouldn't rush in for the score. Rather, he should contain the ball and move into pattern offense.

Now with these rules in mind, the next point of consideration should be that the zone press, like the standard zone, is geared with certain strengths and can be forced into the type of alignment that the offensive team desires. The principles in effect here serve to beat the three trapping defensive principles. These three rules of trapping are depicted in Diagrams 4-27, 28, and 29. If the ball is along the sidelines anywhere on the court, the defense can only be one particular alignment. That alignment is shown in Diagram 4-27. Player 1 has the ball in the back court and is trapped along the sidelines. There are two men on the ball and one man on the same side of the court, one around mid-court and one safety man. This type of alignment is similar on any court sideline. The closer to the basket, the less area the press has to cover.

Any trap that takes place in the center-court area involves two players on the ball, two side-by-side and one back in safety position. This is shown in Diagram 4-28. With 2 possessing the ball and under attack, the alignment of defense is depicted.

Any attack that takes place near or on the baseline is demonstrated in Diagram 4-29 when 2 is trapped by two defensive players and there are two defensive men behind him and one underneath the basket. It is important that these trapping principles are understood, because even with the many traps available defensively, these three rules are in effect.

So what is the implication of the trapping rules? Simply this: if there are only three different types of traps available, then no matter

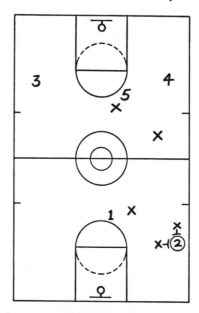

DIAGRAM 4-27
Zone Sideline Trap Principle

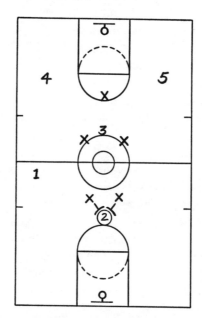

DIAGRAM 4-28
Zone Center-Court Trap Principle

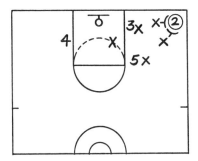

DIAGRAM 4-29
Zone Front-Court Corner Trap Principle

what zone press is used, the offense should be geared to finding loopholes from these particular trap areas. In short, no matter whether the zone press is a two-on-two, a one-two-two, or a one-two-one-one, all presses and alignments when trapping are governed by the three rules mentioned. There are times when players are out of position and may have three men trapping, and they may be in a completely confused state. In this situation, the offense should find the open man in an open area and move the ball up court with less difficulty.

One more point to consider is that there is no disadvantage to the offense through rotation by a zone press. When the zone press rotates, there are still open areas—usually on the weak side away from the ball. If the player with the ball is perceptive, this can serve as an offensive advantage. Generally the players can only rotate clockwise, counterclockwise, or in straight lines to new positions. Still, players move to the particular pressing or rule trapping positions. Once again, offensive players should be taught what to look for in the way of press weaknesses.

Attacking from Zone Traps

In Diagrams 4-30, 4-31, and 4-32 you see the general direction and movements of the ball from zone trap in pressing situations. In Diagram 4-30 with player 2 in a sideline trap, the passing possibilities are outlined. Passes may be short or long. Once a pass is successful, then the fast-break situation should be developed.

In Diagram 4-31 with 2 in a center trap, the passing potential lanes are depicted once again. There are three possible passes with

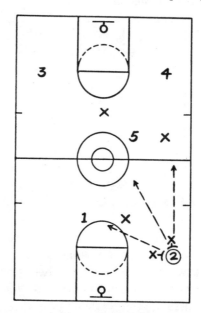

DIAGRAM 4-30
Attacking from Zone Sideline Trap

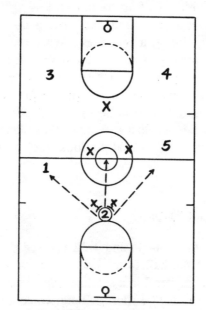

DIAGRAM 4-31
Attacking from Center-Court Trap

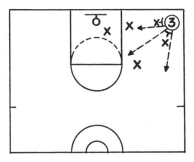

DIAGRAM 4-32
Attacking from Front-Court Corner Trap

only two defenders, which means that someone should be clear and an offensive thrust can be started. In 4-32 the corner trap is shown, as well as the passing lanes and the open areas to pass. The wave attack is used when escaping traps if the regular attack has been throttled. The player possessing the ball (after receiving a pass from the trapped teammate) moves to the basket and looks for a front-court fast-break alignment.

One word about the new versions of combination full-court pressure evolving out of a mixture between man-for-man and zone theories: these defenses may be conquered with the type of attack described. It is possible to organize and find open shooting areas.

Keeping these principles in mind will make it easier for the coach to understand the system.

COACHING GUIDELINES

1. If a defense is standard and gives no pressure, the attack should run through, then around the opponent.
2. If the man-to-man pressure defense picks the offense up at mid-court, it is the ideal position to begin the Cut-and-Slash attack.
3. Insist on player movement to confuse the opponent while opening avenues of scoring.
4. Be alert to the wave attack. Do not force this wave attack, but be alert to its possibility in all the offense.
5. Attempt to get inside a tight man-to-man defense. Go inside, then outside, the sagging man-to-man defenses.
6. In attacking combination and zone defenses, movement of

the men can be in clocking motion. Reversing inside is also possible.

7. If a player is stuck with the basketball, reverses must take place so he may make a successful pass.

8. Basically the theory of attacking zone defenses is to follow the rules which force the zone into the alignment you want and then attack from there.

9. If the ball is passed around the outside of the zone, always be concerned with the possible cut into an open lane.

10. Against pressure defenses, either get the ball in quickly or wait until the players have lined up in preparation for the attack.

11. Try to make the longest available pass first; then go to the short pass. Be alert to make a long pass after a short one.

12. Zone presses under attack can be forced into three general trap rules.

13. Remember that the zone press always is vulnerable on the weak side. Be ready to take advantage of this.

14. When attacking for the shot, at the end of the offense against the zone press, be alert not to force the ball when the defense is in good retreat position.

15. Always know whether the pressure defense is a zone drop-back or a man-to-man drop-back.

5

Setting Up
the Cut-and-Slash Attack

With comprehension of the principles involved in the Cut-and-Slash Attack, it is evident that there should be one more step discussed prior to examining the offensive options. The principles laid the foundation for each option against the various types of defenses. Now an explanation must be made as to how players line up to begin the attack. As in any offensive attack, alignment is important and must be defined. Some of the points to consider are the initial type of the alignment, alignment against different defenses, the movement of players into the alignment, and player responsibilities.

Players just don't materialize into certain positions on the floor. They must move there from any number of former positions. In other words, there is a multitude of combinations relative to player location on defense, but once the ball is secured the players must move into proper offensive alignments, ready to attack.

The aggressive type of ball my teams have played induces many fast-break attacks. The discussion here does not deal with the fast-break attack necessarily, but with occurrences that take place when there are no fast-break possibilities or when there is a delay in the game, allowing for defensive setup. The concern is for moving into position, ready to begin the attack—whether it be from the deep back court, the ten-second line, or the front court.

The Low Post Alignment

In this particular setup, thinking is in terms of play after the guards have brought the ball up and are just over mid-court to the ideal Cut-and-Slash area. The low-post alignment may be used against any type of zone or man-to-man defense. Although the low post is used on occasions in the actual options attack, its primary value is in wave attacking. The middle is left open until the team is set to plunge into an option cut. The individual move charge is more effective with an open three-second lane. The high post takes precedence once the option cut starts. Basically the starting guards line up in the normal guard positions and the starting forwards in the actual forward lane positions, with the starting center in the center position. Flexibility is possible, however, and the guards or forwards can be rotated. An exchange of position between the forwards and the pivot man may take place, too.

My teams have seldom had a lot of height at the pivot position. Consequently, it was found feasible to train big men to play any of the front positions. In fact, some of our most adept pivot scorers have been forwards flashing into the post position. Interchanging positions is desirable and is very effective with versatile players.

Diagram 5-1 shows the basic alignment from the ideal area against zone or man-to-man defenses. Player 5, the pivot man, plays at a low post opposite the ball and about seven feet from the baseline and just outside the three-second area. Three and 4, the forwards, play

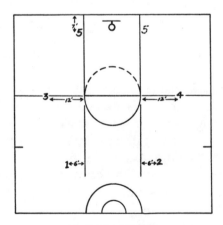

DIAGRAM 5-1
Ideal Low Post Alignment

even with the foul line extended and about 12 feet from the circle. One and 2 play five feet inside the forwards.

Each player positioned is for maximum efficiency in the attack. The guards, 1 and 2, are inside the forwards because they have quicker movements to the basket from that area. The forwards, 3 and 4, play out wide initially to allow movements inside. Opponents therefore tend to leave the inside cutting area open. The pivot man stays low to keep the middle area open and also to be available should a cutter break through the defense in the three-second area for a two-on-one attack in close to the basket with the open cutter.

High Post Alignment

Everything is the same in this alignment except that the pivot man plays at the high post rather than the low post. This opens up a different avenue of scoring. Whereas in the low post we are looking for an open middle and a possible two-on-one with a baseline pivot man, in this offensive attack we are looking to break a cutter loose with all defensive men away from the basket. If a cutter breaks loose, he plays one-on-one against his defensive man within ten feet of the basket, since all other players are at least at a high post position or forward position. The option starts from the high post alignment.

In Diagram 5-2, the high post alignment is shown with the high post man, 5, either in the center of the free-throw circle or on the right

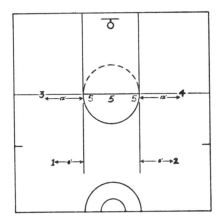

DIAGRAM 5-2
Ideal High Post Alignment

or left side. The position is dictated by the offense in effect or sometimes just strictly by movements on an offensive player's part to secure
a good firm position at the high post. All of the other players are
positioned identically, as in the low post attack.

Diagram 5-3 shows the different paths of movement each player
may take. For example, 1 can go straight to the baseline, move on a

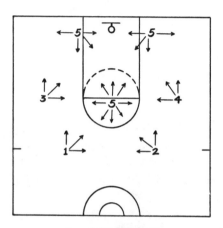

DIAGRAM 5-3
Player Movement Paths from High or Low Post Alignments

diagonal line across the three-second lane, or move toward 2. Three
has choices of coming toward 1, to the free-throw line, to the basket or
the baseline. Five in a low post can move toward the sideline or up
towards the foul line or across the front of the basket to the foul line.
Five in the high post position has more movement because he is in the
center court area.

Player direction paths are important to learn, because there are
coordinated efforts on each player's part when attacking, so consequently each player must know in what direction he can move.

Player Responsibility

The player responsibilities are listed to describe the relevancy of
the alignment in the attack from half-court.

The responsibilities of each guard are to:

1. Pass to start the offense.
2. Cut to the basket.

3. Free himself to catch a pass by using feints and fakes.
4. Reverse with a forward.
5. Reverse with the other guard.
6. Screen for the slasher and roll in.
7. Stay back on defense.
8. Drive to the basket.
9. Shoot the jumper from outside.

The responsibilities of each forward are to:

1. Free himself to catch a pass, using fakes and feints when necessary.
2. Pass and cut.
3. Pass to a cutter.
4. Slash after a teammate sets a screen.
5. Screen for a teammate to slash.
6. Rebound missed shots.
7. Reverse with a guard.
8. Exchange with the pivot man.
9. Flat-cut to the basket.
10. Execute a screen-and-roll play with a guard or the pivot man.
11. Shoot the jumper from outside.
12. Exchange with the opposite forward.
13. Drive to the basket.

The responsibilities of the pivot-man are to:

1. Free himself to receive a pass, using fakes and feints when necessary.
2. Pass to a cutter.
3. Move out to the corner to jump shoot, drive, or pass to another player—usually inside.
4. Drive to the basket.
5. Exchange with a forward.
6. Screen for a slasher, then roll in.
7. Screen for cutters, then roll in.
8. Look to play two-on-one with a cutter.
9. Rebound missed shots.
10. Screen and roll for a driving forward.
11. Play one-on-one in the internal zone.

One of the guards must assume the responsibility of being quarterback and communicate the game plan with necessary changes. Players may start in the position most convenient once they learn to execute the various responsibilities.

Full-Court Man-for-Man Press Alignment

The full-court man-for-man alignment is a little different from the alignment used against full-court zone pressure. Against man-to-man it is more conducive to effective scoring to position two deep players near the offensive basket. The third player floats in the mid-court vicinity waiting to help out in case the two back guards bringing the ball up have a problem with the defense. Against man-to-man, this alignment setup can be organized very quickly and the attack formulated very efficiently.

My teams have tried using identical alignments against both types of defenses but found that changing the zone alignment is a little more successful to suit their purposes. It was discovered that bringing up another player to mid-court made the zone attack more potent. The advent of the diamond press, which is a formation of the one-two-one-one, forced moving potential receivers into two mid-court positions on either side of the court. Quick, short passes could then be made and weak side (the side away from the ball) could also be worked much more effectively. Consequently, the change was made to adopt two different alignments. The basic attack pattern is almost identical.

Diagram 5-4 shows the basic alignment against man-to-man pressure. One has the ball ready to throw inbounds. Two moves to receive a pass. Four stays near mid-court to the ball side and is ready to move for a pass should this be necessary. He may also start from the other side of the court (identified by the dotted number), while 3 and 5 operate close to the offensive basket.

Diagram 5-5 points out the different types of movements possible to receive passes or to evade the defensive man when attacking. The arrows indicate movement paths. Players' responsibilities incorporate some of those listed in the regular pattern with some variance. The variance refers to moving the ball up-court to a position triggering the option in effect. The responsibilities by player are:

Player 1:

1. Inbounds the ball.

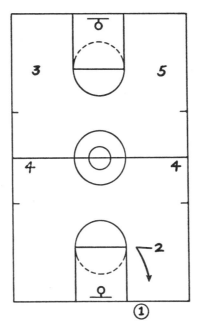

DIAGRAM 5-4
Full-Court Man-to-Man Pressure Alignment

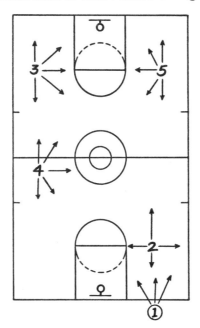

DIAGRAM 5-5
Player Movement Paths Against Full-Court
Man-to-Man Pressure

2. May receive a return pass.
3. Moves to appropriate spot for the offensive thrust, or starts the offense.
4. Follows through with proper offensive team play.

Player 2:

1. Moves to receive inbounds pass.
2. Returns pass to 1 if checked closely, otherwise starts the appropriate offense.
3. May take ball to basket with dribble if the offense breaks down.

Player 3:

1. Helps out if needed to inbound ball.
2. Helps if needed to bring ball up-court.
3. May be a feeder after receiving a pass in the mid-court area.
4. Assumes appropriate place in option.

Players 4 and 5:

1. Exchange positions with each other.
2. Move to receive a pass if needed.
3. Blend properly in the offensive pattern.

Full-Court Zone Press Alignment

The zone press alignment is used against all zone presses that the opposition may attempt to use. The players are positioned to pass the ball ahead and also to pass up-court via the lane of the ball to the middle lane to the weak-side lane. Diagram 5-6 depicts the zone press offensive alignment. One has the ball and is ready to inbound it. Two looks for the pass reception. Three and 4 are positioned just over the mid-court line on either side of the court, while 5 is deep in the offensive and in the circle.

Diagram 5-7 shows the different movement possibilities to initiate an attack. The arrows indicate potential player movements, as well as ball movement.

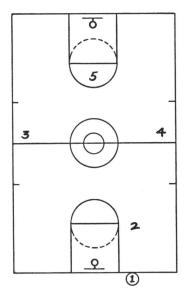

DIAGRAM 5-6
Full-Court Zone Press Alignment

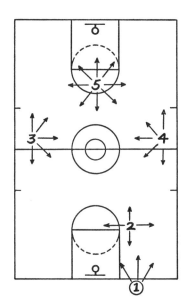

DIAGRAM 5-7
Player Movement Paths Against Full-Court Zone Press

Player responsibilities by number are:

Player 1:

1. Inbound the ball.
2. Pass and go away from the ball.
3. Blend into the offense, or receive the pass, then start the offense.

Player 2:

1. Move to receive the pass inbounds.
2. Look to start the offense or return the ball to 1, then blend into the offense.

Player 3 and 4:

1. Help out if needed to inbound ball.
2. Move to proper offensive spots to blend into pattern.
3. Exchange positions with each other.

Player 5:

1. Moves to receive a long pass near the top of the circle or to a side lane.
2. Blends into proper place in offensive pattern.

Dribbling should be minimized against zone presses except when close to the offensive basket, or if the pattern disintegrates. Whenever a player receives a pass, he should turn, face the offensive basket, then make the appropriate pass or move.

Player Movement into Proper Basic Alignments

Let's consider player movements after the ball is dead. Assuming that on live balls we would be fast-breaking anyway, then the transitional break would go into effect, followed by the pattern offense. However, movements to the proper positions when the ball is dead need scrutiny at this time. Along with movements on the dead ball, the concern is with getting into the alignments from deep in the back-court area. Anytime we get the ball out of bounds in the front-court area, we set up an out-of-bounds play and make quick charging thrusts at the basket.

The first alignment follows after an opponent's basket. Players at that time could be scattered in defensive areas. Basically, we want to get the ball to one of the better ball handlers while allowing the other players to race into the offensive alignments.

Diagram 5-8 shows player 1 passing the ball to player 2, moving toward the pass. Player 3 moves to the left side to his proper position.

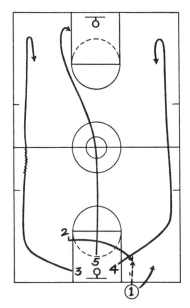

DIAGRAM 5-8
Setting Up Offensive Alignment Following Opponent's Basket

Five moves up-court to the low post, and player 4 moves directly up the right lane to the right side forward position. Player 1 makes the pass to player 2 and moves inbounds. With these movements, players are in position and ready to formally start the offense.

There are other times that ball may be dead, permitting the defense to set up. Consequently, the attack must occur in orderly fashion. These situations might occur after a made free throw, after a violation by the opponent, or after a turnover by the opponent. In the next three diagrams, I will describe three different ways to move out of a defensive position and into the offensive alignments following any of these delays.

Diagram 5-9 depicts movement after a regular free-throw defense is set up followed by the successful free throw. The defense alignment

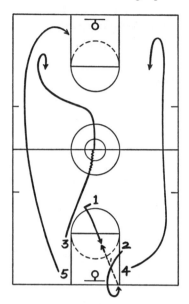

DIAGRAM 5-9
Setting Up Offensive Alignment Following Successful Free Throw

is a box type with one player located at the top of the circle. He can move in several directions, including to the ball. The diagram shows 2 moving out-of-bounds to pick up the ball. Four moves to the right side into proper position. Five moves to the left side into his position. Three moves towards the middle area and up toward the center court, where he slows down, looks, then moves to the regular offensive position. One moves inside the foul line ready to receive a pass.

Players running up-court must do so while watching the ball. They should always be aware of the ensuing action. It is also important for the designated player to act as third man in case of problems with entering or moving the ball up-court, and to be available for help in case of excessive pressure. He makes a change of pace near mid-court and looks to help out. If not needed, this player assumes his regular position. The player inbounding the ball may have difficulty due to pressure on the other player trying to get loose to receive the pass, creating a necessity for the delay by the third player, who could help by screening for the loose guard or by receiving a pass himself. This protects against a violation by the player trying to inbound the ball.

Diagram 5-10 depicts the play action after the successful free throw, but with a big man taking the ball out instead of a smaller man.

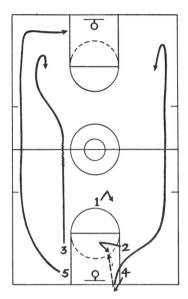

DIAGRAM 5-10
Setting Up Alignment with Tall Player
Inbounding Successful Free Throw

The big man, 4, moves to the basket to secure the successful shot, then takes the ball out of bounds in readiness to pass inbounds. Two moves into position to get the pass, and 1 heads up toward mid-court, then doubles back, while 5 races up-court along the left sidelines, as does 3. Four makes the pass-in, then sprints up-court. This play gives a lot of movement, but again it gets the players into the desired positions.

Diagram 5-11 shows a little more movement to lend confusion to the defense. This takes place when 2 takes the ball after the free throw is made. Five crosses over from the left side of the court to the right side, continuing to the low post position. Four crosses from the right side of the court to the left side and assumes that forward position up-court, while 1 moves into position to receive a pass from 2. Meanwhile, 3 speeds up-court just left of the center lane, delays, then moves to his starting position, which in this case is the left forward. These various movements can be effective in helping players secure offensive positions as well as to loosen the defense enough to allow the ball to be thrown inbounds.

When a violation occurs, the ball may be put in play along either sideline, anywhere from the baseline to mid-court. The concern here is to enter the ball in a position to make a thrust to the basket. We can

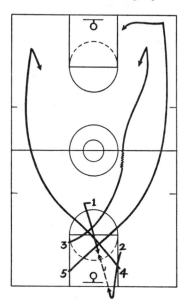

DIAGRAM 5-11
Setting Up Offensive with Player Crossing Movements

make this thrust because of the delay on violations, allowing time for the alignment to be developed.

Diagram 5-12 shows the play in action. One takes the ball out on the sideline in the back court and passes it to 2. Five fans out to the left sideline and moves to his position. Four moves to his position. Three starts moving, changes pace to look to help out if necessary, then speeds up-court to his position on the left side.

Diagram 5-13 shows a variation with the big man inbounding the ball to a little man, with the proper play sequence. Player 4 throws the ball inbounds to player 1. Player 2 delays in the back-court to help out if needed. Player 3 moves to his position, while 5 moves up the right sideline to his position. Player 4, after making the inbounds pass, rapidly moves to his up-court position.

Alignment effectiveness is increased by the speed of a player moving up-court, by his looking inside toward the ball, and by the change of pace and ready position for the designated player, in case he is needed to help the ball handlers out prior to moving up-court. These fundamentals make it possible to get into option positions rapidly and efficiently whenever there is no fast breaking. Efficient movement to alignments presents smoother offensing with more scoring potential.

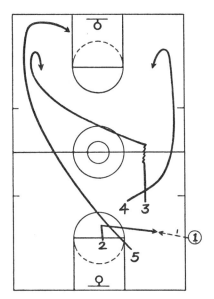

DIAGRAM 5-12
Setting Up Alignment with Small Player Inbounding Ball from Back-Court Sidelines

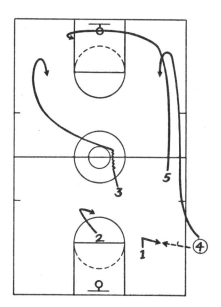

DIAGRAM 5-13
Setting Up Alignment with Tall Player Inbounding Ball from Back-Court Sidelines

ANALYZING PERSONNEL

In thinking of the personnel for the Cut-and-Slash attack, we find that there are many ways to utilize the players. For a player to be really effective, it is essential that he become versatile in all aspects of the game. Offensively he must develop a large assortment of moves with or without the ball, drives with the ball, and shots. The footwork development comes into play with stopping, changing directions, and changing of speeds. A large portion of practice time is spent developing players to fulfill their role in the attack. Basically, using the two smaller and presumably more agile players in the guard positions may be better for cutting purposes, while the bigger players playing the forward positions or pivot position may be more effective as slashers.

However, since versatility has been stressed in team play with a mobile attack, a good deal of success has been with players fitting in at any position. Of course the player bringing the ball up-court must be an adept ball handler. Any player racing up-court may fill any available spot without hurting the offense. It has been noted on many occasions that a tall player can be an excellent cutter. Captain Bill Brown of the Windsor University team was 6'3 ½" tall and built muscularly. He was quite versatile and possessed excellent basketball sense, along with footwork skills. Bill scored at least two baskets a game strictly by getting involved in the guard position, making a pass and sprinting up the middle after a change of pace to outwit and outrun taller defenders. It was uncanny how often Bill ended up all alone under the basket. This tactic helped Bill make All-Canadian in his senior year while leading the team to the National Championship.

Several years later, Angelo Mazzuchin, the fine All-Canadian Guard and captain for Windsor University, at 6'1" possessed many refined pivot moves, along with being tough, aggressive and strong around the backboard. We found that with Angelo playing one of the forward positions, he could on occasion move into the pivot and use one of his many shots to shoot over his defensive guard. As a side benefit, Angelo was able to rebound a missed shot and make his second effort, due to his strength and jumping ability.

Revolving men from the pivot or forward positions can often be very useful, since it takes big strong defensive players away from the backboards. In man-to-man defense, tall players may not move as agilely as the offensive man. This may play havoc with the opponent. Such versatility can give a team a great advantage.

USE OF SUBSTITUTES

We have advocated the rule of developing basketball players to play basketball. The aim and intent of this is to play all the boys that are on the ball club, rather than to develop "splinter-catchers," or observers. The boys on the team are selected to play basketball games, and they are active basketball players. When we talk about playing a game, we are implying that all ten or 12 boys (whichever number we dress) are going to participate in the game. Since the Cut-and-Slash is a pressure, go-go type of offense, and combining it with the rest of the pressing, running game makes it practically impossible for a player to perform in all of the game's aspects without rest, it is necessary that athletes be in superb condition. Also, the strain of this type of running game demands that substitutes be used. Substitutes have played a major role in helping my teams win championships year in and year out. There have been many games where an observer can't distinguish a starting player from a substitute player. In fact, rarely have these teams gone more than two or three games without shifting the starting lineup. When a Cut-and-Slash team arrives at a gym to play basketball, it is arriving to play the game with all of the players. No matter what players start the game, all will play a major role in the contest.

Some of the ideas advocated in using substitutes are:

1. It is important that all players participate in the first half of the game. It is unfair to expect a boy to come off the bench in the last few minutes of a pressure-packed game to perform at top capacity. Consequently, every player should play early in the game.
2. Anytime a ball player tires and shows signs of not being able to keep up with the game tempo, he should be replaced with a substitute, even if it means taking out an outstanding player. A tired, excellent player is only mediocre whereas a mediocre, hustling, rested player may be excellent.
3. A coach should try not to substitute more than two boys at a time. He should allow a few minutes for these two to warm up before sending in other players.
4. A player entering the game should race up and down the court with emphasis on defense and rebounding along with pattern playmaking rather than on trying to set up a shot for himself. He shouldn't force a shot; rather, he should let the

natural sequence of play avail him shooting chances. Meanwhile, he warms up to the play situation as well as warming up physically.

5. Allow substitutes to play for several minutes rather than removing them immediately. Short time periods don't really offer a player a fair chance to perform up to capacity.
6. In the second half, keep substitutes in the game who had a hot scoring hand, were rebounding well, or just generally contributed to successful team play.
7. Play the second half according to important situations with the players executing at top efficiency; substitute according to excessive fouls, erratic playing, or tired players.

Soon players perceive that in the fast, aggressive game, they must always be ready to step right into the game with emotional and physical readiness, prepared to assume the required role with little warning. Boys enjoy playing this kind of basketball, and it helps team cohesion and performance when each realizes that he will participate and make his contribution to the game.

This player participation plan has been successful both on the high school and the college level. Teams must build a bench.

COACHING GUIDELINES

1. It is important to realize the value of a properly aligned attack, using minimum time.
2. Ideally, guards can bring the ball up-court, forwards can play their regular positions, and the post man may play high or low.
3. Actually, any player may move into any position before starting the attack.
4. Two players should go deep against man-to-man pressure defense. The third man up-court will always change pace near mid-court in order to be available to help inbound the ball.
5. Make sure the zone press offensive alignment is spread out a little more than the man-to-man.
6. A player should sprint past the desired spot, then double back, ready to move and free himself for a pass.

7. Either big or small players may take the ball out of bounds, provided they have an opportunity to practice this fundamental often.
8. Versatile players have more opportunities to score.
9. The bench can be the difference in winning championships or running out of gas late in the season.
10. Substitutes need playing time to develop physical prowess, poise, and confidence.

6

The X Attack
in the Cut-and-Slash

Up to this point the involvement of the Cut-and-Slash attack has been reviewed. This has included analysis of various parts of the attack, the principles and components involved, and also the methods of pattern alignment. Now it is appropriate to explain in totality the six different options forming the Cut-and-Slash Attack. The primary difference in each option is distinguished by the cutting and slashing phases. Each attack is given a specific name. The balance wheel and weak-side slashes blend into any of the six options without a change in characteristics. The option cutting phase is employed against all of the defenses, whereas the slashing phase is adapted against both man-for-man basic and pressure defenses. Each option will be explained thoroughly as to the mechanics against the various types of defenses, ranging from half-court basic defenses to full-court presses. To explain this point a little farther, the basic cut will be similar in each attack against any defenses, but except for the man-to-man attack, there is not a definite four-step program (see page 37), since zone movement is a little different, as explained in Chapter 4. Cuts and various slashes are still used, but the rotation system is a little different for more effective attacking.

The same explanation is in order for the full-court man-to-man attack. The cutting is similar initially against this defense, but the sequence does not necessarily take place in proper cut, slash, balance wheel, weak-side slash order. The attack's success does not rely on involvement of the four steps.

This is also the case against zone pressure defenses. It is not necessary to use all four parts to attack, because it is conducive to score with the initial movement. If there is no basket available, set the alignment properly to commence with the half-court regular zone offense.

Another point to be re-emphasized here is that the balance wheel step may take place either in its proper sequence or any time the offense has reached a point of deterioration. If for some reason there is a breakdown in an offensive pattern, the balance wheel may take place, ideally followed by inside slashing or the weak-side attack against man-for-man defense. Consequently it may be necessary to revert to the balance wheel to either start weak-side attacking or to start the offense all over again. Also remember the individual movement for shots originating from the balance wheel attack.

Option I, the X Attack, allows for double cutters on the initial movement and sets the focus on the middle-court lane area. Attacking the middle lane gives the option of moving forward to the basket or moving either to the left or the right while keeping away from corner areas. In this, as in all the options, the cutters move straight to the basket with the idea of initially working to the basket and then starting to slash on angles. The purpose is to avoid lateral types of offensive movements with the ball that are easier to defend against. It also forces the defense to move back closer to the basket, and it is easier to take shots in the internal area.

Attacking Man-for-Man Defenses

The X Attack initiates off a high post. A guard passes to the post man; then both guards cut to the basket.

Diagram 6-1 shows the X Attack. Two has the ball and passes to 5. Two then makes a fake to his right and breaks off 5. Two then makes a fake to his right and breaks off 5 and goes to the basket. One fakes to his left and cuts off the post man to the right side, giving a criss-cross off the post man. Four and 3 fake toward the basket and come back to position just off the top of the circle.

The shots available here are lay-ups, after a pass from 5 by either 1 or 2, or short jump shots by 3 or 4 near the top of the circle. Also, a drive or jump shot by the post man is an excellent possibility.

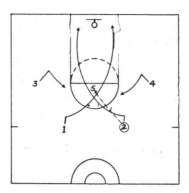

DIAGRAM 6-1
X Attack Against Man-to-Man Defense

Diagram 6-2 is a second type of cut off a criss-cross formation. In this cut, even though it is referred to as an X cut, both 1 and 2 fake the criss-cross and go straight to the basket. In the diagram, 2 passes the ball to 5 and is the first cutter, and 1 follows. Three and 4 make the identical movement as in the first play. This variation is used to catch teams sleeping, or overplaying and switching trying to cut the path to the basket.

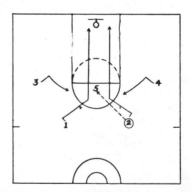

DIAGRAM 6-2
Fake Criss-Cross Attack Against Man-to-Man Defense

The slashes are effective because the two big men (forwards) back under the basket and the guards back out to shooting positions near the top of the circle. There is actually no planned contact on the cuts. There is planned contact in the slashing movement. The two big men

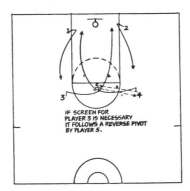

IF SCREEN FOR
PLAYER 3 IS NECESSARY
IT FOLLOWS A REVERSE PIVOT
BY PLAYER 5.

DIAGRAM 6-3
X Attack Basic Slash Against Man-to-Man Defense

moving in toward the basket hook up opponents on the post man. This tactic off the slash screens the defensive man to free the cutter.

In Diagram 6-3, 5 passes the ball out to 4. If there is no shot possible, 4 returns it to 5 and then with a slight fake to the right comes around 5 to the left. Five pivots into the path of 4's defensive man, trying to free 4. If 4 is picked up by 5's defensive man, 5 goes to the basket. If this is not possible, 3 cuts off 5, who then reverse-pivots into 3's defensive man's path, allowing 3 to become an open man moving toward the basket. Either 3 or 4 is clear for a lay-up, or in many instances, 5 is free to move in with the ball on the switch-off for an easy lay-up. Meanwhile, 1 and 2 move back to shooting areas near the top of the circle.

One thing that should be noted here is that passes or handoffs should not be made by the post man until the cutter is close to the basket. When a cutter clears the post man and gets loose near the basket, there is less opportunity to have the defensive post opponent steal a pass or handoff. It's also more difficult for him to block shots.

A second type of slash off the X Attack is shown in Diagram 6-4. After the initial cut by 1 and 2, 3 and 4 have no shot, but the ball is passed out to 4, who then returns the ball to the post man, 5. At this time 3 and 4 move directly in to screen for 1 and 2. Since 4 passed the ball, he screens first for 2, who moves behind the screen for a pass and shot. If he's not clear, 1 quickly makes the same move off the screen by 3. Five may pass to 2 for a jump shot, to 4 for a lay-up, to 1 for a jumper or to 3 for a lay-up—in that sequence. If nothing happens, the lane should open to allow 5 to drive or look for a jump shot.

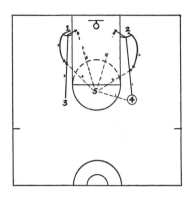

DIAGRAM 6-4
X Attack and Second Type Slash Against Man-to-Man Defense

If nothing has taken place up to now, the balance wheel is formed. In Diagram 6-5, assume that 4 ended up with the ball and couldn't shoot, so he passes out to 1. Meanwhile, 2 forms the balance wheel in accordance with the principle of balancing the floor by running over to the left top spot, 3 moves out to the right top spot, 5 moves to the low right spot, while 4 stays at the low post.

Diagram 6-6 shows the balance wheel offense set-up and a play. One play that has worked beautifully for us through the years is a simple reverse to get the pivot man back into the post area. Four breaks over to replace 5. Five sets an outside screen just outside the lane at the low post. In the diagram, 1 passes the ball to 2, who passes to 3, who passes to 4 for a jump shot or a pass to 5 at the low post. This reverse play either clears 4 for a shot or 5 for a one-on-one underneath the basket, or a shot.

In the balance wheel, it is essential always to alert to hit a man at the low post and allow him to go one-on-one, since this is an excellent method of attack. This puts pressure on the defense by penetrating internally.

The weak-side slash play off the balance wheel is shown in Diagram 6-7. Four has the ball and drives off 5 for a pick-and-roll play, with 5 rolling to the basket for a shot. (A point to remember: All of the weak-side slash plays may be used with any option, even though a different play will be depicted with each option.)

With all these plays, the three men nearest to the backboard rebound while the two men nearest the foul line stay back as defensive players.

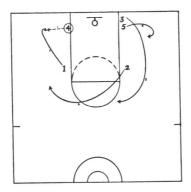

DIAGRAM 6-5
Balance Wheel from X Attack

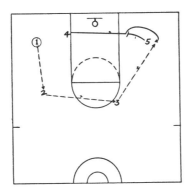

DIAGRAM 6-6
Balance Wheel Pivot Man and Forward Simple Screen and Reverse

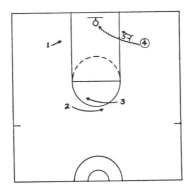

DIAGRAM 6-7
Weak-Side Slash Pick-and-Roll Play

Attacking Zone Defenses

The first option cut can be effective against zone defenses, even though this seems to violate the thinking of many coaches. The thought is that criss-crossing has no effect against a zone because of stationary area coverage. However, we have found it to be extremely helpful to use this attack—not with the idea of hooking men up on the post man, but rather with the idea of cutting to the basket looking for a surprise quick pass and a little easy shot. Also, along with this movement, of course, it is easy to set up the attack.

Diagram 6-8 shows 2 with the ball passing to 5. Without faking, 2 cuts directly to the basket from right to left. One, without faking, cuts

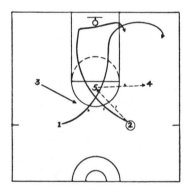

DIAGRAM 6-8
X Attack Against Zones

directly to the right side and down the lane. With these cuts it is important that both men look to weave their way into the deep internal area to surprise the defensive men underneath the basket, the thought being that often a sudden stop followed by a pass can be highly successful for a lay-up or a one-on-one situation in the deep zone.

Windsor University's Bobby Horvath, Joe Green, and Ed Petryshyn did well at cutting and weaving inside the zone while catching quick passes for lay-ups against basic zones.

In Diagram 6-8, after the cutting, the setup is developed for the zone offense and clocking movements that have been discussed in Chapter 4. Note that 1 is in the corner, 4 at the foul-line position, 2 is at the low post, 3 is at the top of the circle, while 5 is in the post position. Five passes out to 4 to key to start the offense.

Attacking Full-Court Man-for-Man Pressure

The X Attack can be extremely effective against full-court man-to-man pressure defenses by opening opportunities off the criss-cross, or by moving to a fast-break situation. Ideally, look to move in as quickly as possible to score. One of the vital components of scoring against presses is the need for total organization at the end of the press offense. In other words, when the ball is passed close to the basket, the team must be completely organized to be effective as a scoring unit. If nothing materializes, move to the basic starting position and attack the man-to-man drop-back defense with the appropriate four-step movements.

Diagram 6-9 shows the attack against man-to-man pressure defense. The alignment used is always the same as described earlier. One and 2 are in the back court. Three stands at mid-court, while 4 and the pivot man, 5, are up near the top of the circle.

In Diagram 6-9, 1 throws the ball inbounds to 2, who passes to 3. (Three has moved to position on the ball side of the ten-second area.) It is important that the 3 man never stand on the ten-second line. Both 1 and 2 fake and cut to the basket while 4 and 5 move towards mid-court.

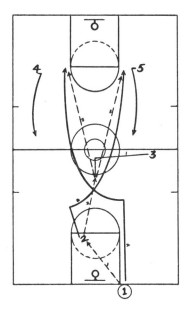

DIAGRAM 6-9
X Attack Against Full-Court Man-to-Man Pressure

Available shots here follow a pass to 1 or 2 cutting for the basket. Again, rather than handoffs, longer passes are preferred because the cutters usually break through the traffic where the ball is located and find themselves close to the basket, ready to dribble after receiving a pass. Four and 5 move out to mid-court area and follow 1 and 2 to become forwards. If it is indicated that either 1 or 2 isn't going to shoot, then 4 and 5 move toward the basket and exchange positions with 1 and 2 to prepare for a follow-up attack. If nothing develops, it is conceivable that the play must stop. A balance wheel could take place, followed by the weak-side slash, omitting the first two offensive steps. The movements are designed for considerable latitude and freedom on the court.

Attacking Zone Pressure

Even against zone pressure, cutters on the first option pattern can still be used. The movement will not hamper the zone attack in any way. It is seen again, as against zones, that the movements off a post serve to keep players heading toward the basket and allow them to set up in position to receive a pass to continue the pattern and descend to a shooting area.

An example of this is in Diagram 6-10. It shows 1 passing the ball to 2; 2 passes to 3 at mid-court. Three passes to 5, who is at the foul line for a fast-break alignment. Two is on the left wing, and 4 is on the right wing with 1 occupying the trailer position. If nothing develops, the regular zone offense is set up.

In beating zone presses, it is important to take the ball in to score, to pass more than dribble, to avoid trap situations and to escape from trap situations. Also, it is vital to exploit the weak side.

All zones are the same in trapping situations. If trapped, then with knowledge of the basic escape movements, pass out to attack the opposite side of the court. Of course, fast-break organization takes place after this movement. It is better to avoid being trapped. Passing the ball up the court and keeping organized in making the attempt to score at the end with complete style is the goal.

The X Attack in its entirety against all defenses is a grinding type which offers many scoring opportunities with freedom in the movements, as well as several cuts and slashes freeing players moving toward the basket over and over again.

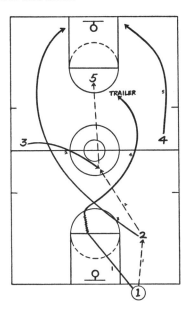

DIAGRAM 6-10
X Attack Against Full-Court Zone Pressure

COACHING GUIDELINES

1. On the initial pass to the post man against man-to-man defenses, the player passing the ball should cut first.
2. Cutters should cross under the basket to the opposite side of the court if they don't receive a pass.
3. The forwards moving out should always remain in a shooting area while the cutting is taking place, ready to take the 16- or 18-foot jumper.
4. The pivot man is extremely important, because he becomes a real threat to go one-on-one near the basket, particularly against the man-to-man defense.
5. In the slashing movements, have the passer first screen for the slasher while the opposite slasher is second.
6. In the balance wheel, always keep the players as close to the basket as possible in order to shoot quickly, when possible.
7. One-on-one may be very possible off the balance wheel.
8. When attacking a full-court press defense, use criss-crossing, but do not pass the ball off until the cutters break loose close to the basket.

9. Remember that organization is essential at the end of the press offense.
10. When attacking the zone press, avoid the dribble and be ready to pass the ball up-court to players in open court space.
11. Try to stay out of trapped areas when moving up-court. Keep the players spread out to avoid congesting a small court area.

7

The Cut-and-Slash
Replacement Attack

The second option to be examined is the Replacement Attack. This option is chiefly executed in a side lane when the thrust begins, but the ball is brought to the three-second lane in the final stage for the shots. There is player movement to the ball similar to the clocking movements used against zone defenses with pressure exerted on the defensive man to move away from the basket whenever protecting with a man-for-man defense. Eventually one of the offensive players secures a low post position or a high post fast-break position. In the low post position, the player plays one-on-one against his opponent, while in the high post position, he looks for a fast-break tandem attack. This tandem attack also includes a trailer in proper position, ready to strike. The value of the second option lies in drawing players away from the basket while players moving clockwise or counterclockwise may move into excellent offensive position near the basket. Since a versatile player has numerous available tactics against an individual defensive man, conceivably he should have many opportunities to score. The Replacement Attack is very practical in offensing full-court pressure defenses, by attacking one lane with offensive players moving as close to the ball as necessary to get clear for a pass reception with the attack terminating in the internal zone.

The cutters in this option originate from the weak side of the court, move to the basket area, and then go to the strong side for utilization as pass receivers and play-makers. The first object is to beat the defensive man to the basket for a score, the second choice is to secure a post position, and the third choice is to clock to the lane of the ball, setting up for a pass reception and remaining ready to continue the offense from that point.

Slashing takes place involving two players at a time. One weak-side player screens for the other, then follows with a roll-in. Meanwhile, this is repeated by two other players on the strong side of the court. The first pair maneuver for the slash in the original weak-side lane. If there is no shot, the second twosome screen and slash ball-side. While this maneuvering takes place, the player with the ball in a post position readies for a drive, shot, or pass prior to passing off the ball. Internal scoring is quite evident in the Replacement option. The balance wheel and weak-side slash follow if shots don't materialize after the first two steps.

Attacking Man-for-Man Defenses

Naturally, the Replacement Attack may originate in the right or left side lane with either back court player serving as the dominant force in starting the play. The basic cut of the Replacement is shown in Diagram 7-1. This particular play involves three passes to reach the post man. Sometimes a Replacement play may involve four or five passes, depending upon the defensive pressure by the players guarding the pass receivers. Four moves toward 2 to receive a pass, while 5

DIAGRAM 7-1
Replacement Attack Against Man-to-Man Defense

moves from a low post position to receive a pass from 4 in the right lane, and 3 takes the high post position and receives a pass from 5. Five then breaks for the basket while 1 has moved to the basket in a left wing position. This forms a tandem between 1, 3, and 4. Four moves to the top of the circle (and may be used as a trailer), while 2 moves to the left outside position. If 3 assumed the low post position, then he could play one-on-one from that position in the internal zone. The other players fill in the rebounding and defensive spots. Shots available from the high post position attack are from 1, 5, or 3, while 4 could also be a shooter by using the trailer moves—either inside or outside of the tandem.

When the offensive players move out to catch a pass, the defensive player must move out also. If the defense doesn't challenge the pass, then the offense originates close to the internal zone. This is especially confusing to the defense, and both movements benefit the offense. Weak-side action really comes into its own from this attack, too, because of floor balancing by players moving away from the ball. Defensive players often are guilty of looking at the ball, thus allowing their offensive man to break clear to the basket. One of the classiest examples of successful Replacing was seen against a strong Buffalo University team. Windsor University hadn't beaten the Bulls for three years and was trailing late in the third quarter. The Windsor team was smothered by the Bulls' tight, rugged man-for-man basic and pressure defense. The Replacement was installed—with amazing results! Time after time Buffalo's big men were pulled away from the boards and outnumbered with fast-break alignments to shave the 15-point deficit. Finally at one point Windsor scored 20 consecutive points to take a ten-point lead, then played basket exchange to win by ten points in a major upset.

If there is no shot off the cuts and fast-break alignment, then the slashing takes place with reverse movements. Players near the backboards move out to set screens for those outside.

This is similar to the slashes in the X Attack, except that the center man keeps ball possession, an inside screen is used, the slash on the weak side takes place first, and slashing may take place from further away from the basket. In Diagram 7-2, slashing is depicted. Three has the ball with no pass available. One moves to screen inside for 2, then rolls in after 2 passes him. Both players move to the left side if there is no shot, then 5 screens for 4 to slash, and 5 rolls in after that

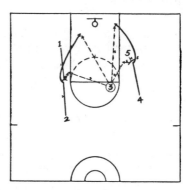

DIAGRAM 7-2
Replacement Attack Slash Against Man-to-Man Defense

move is made. There are several shot possibilities, as well as rebounders moving into good position.

To form the balance wheel off this attack, whoever happens to get
stuck with the ball with no shot passes out to the closest available
player. The other players fill in the wheel.

In Diagram 7-3, assuming that 4 received the pass and couldn't
shoot, 4 passes to 2 in the low left spot. Two passes to 3 at the top left.
Three moves into position on the right side of the court, and 4, after
passing the ball out, moves to the right side—allowing 5 to take a low
post position. This sets up the next step of attack if no thrust was made.

In Diagram 7-4 the weak-side slash takes place. This particular

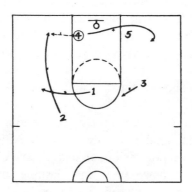

DIAGRAM 7-3
Balance Wheel from the Replacement

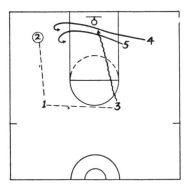

DIAGRAM 7-4
Weak-Side Slash Clear-Out Play

play demonstrates the potential driving moves of a player with the ball. It is a clear-out, one-on-one attack performed by 4 and 5 clearing out the right side of the court and allowing ball handler 3 to make a one-on-one drive. Remember, it was mentioned earlier that one of the finest plays in basketball is still the dribble-in and dribble-out. A player dribbling to the basket and finding himself without a shot can also dribble out while facing the basket and shoot or make a pass underneath to a man at the low post. This diagrammed clear-out play may be used in any option off the balance wheel, as mentioned in Chapter 6.

Attacking Zone Defenses

Once again the attack with a replacement option sets up the players to move to the regular zone attack, which emphasizes the clocking features. The replacement players are already in a clocking type of movement, so it is very easy to move right into the zone offense.

In Diagram 7-5, the zone offense takes place when 2 starts the replacement attack with a pass to 4, who can move up as far as he wants to start the offense. In this case he moves up just beyond the circle. Five, starting from a low post position, moves to the right wing position for a pass from 4. Three assumes the pivot and 1 goes down to the right corner. Two moves to the right low post and 4 takes the outside position to complete the offensive alignment in readiness for the clocking attack. Occasionally a pass to 3 or 2 sets up the shot off the cutting.

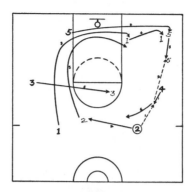

DIAGRAM 7-5
Replacement Attack Against Zones

Attacking Full-Court Man-to-Man Pressure

The Replacement option is ideal for attacking full-court man-to-man pressure defenses. Concentrating in the same lane of the court in this particular option is a safe method of attacking. Generally speaking, by progressing on the same side of the court and then moving to the middle area in attacking a man-to-man pressure defense, a team seems to have fewer violations and fewer bad passes and interceptions by the defense.

By spreading the offensive men over the whole court and having movement toward the ball in a replacement style, we enable men to spring loose in the other two lanes and move in for easy lay-ups time after time. Of course there are times that opponents realize the action trend. They move defensive big men away from the basket area. They counter this movement by dropping off the offensive players moving out to catch a pass. This defeats the purpose of the press, enabling us to bring the ball up-court with relative ease.

An example of the attack against man-to-man pressure is shown in Diagram 7-6. One passes the ball inbounds to 2, who passes the ball to 4, who is replacing toward the ball. This play originates off the man-to-man full-court alignment. After 4 receives the pass, he turns and faces the basket and anticipates a man replacing or filling his previous position—which in this case is 5. Meanwhile, 3 moves from the weak side to replace 5 and is available for the pass. Three passes to 1 at the foul line. Two is at the weak-side wing position. Three takes the strong-side wing position after making a pass to 1, and 5 moves in the

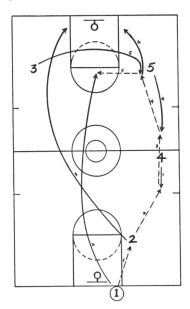

DIAGRAM 7-6
Replacement Attack Against Full-Court Man-to-Man Pressure

trailer position. Finally, with this fast-break alignment, once the ball is inside the foul-line area, 3 with the ball has the option to dribble to the basket, too. If the ball is moved to the middle lane at mid-court, it may be dribbled to the basket—especially by a fast, outstanding ball handler.

Attacking Full-Court Zone Pressure

Zone presses come in many varieties and have different types of trapping theories, but, as we stated earlier, there are only three different trapping alignments. Regardless of what the press looks like, there are still only three trapping principles involved, so as long as we do one of two things, attacking pressure can be simplified. First, it is of primary importance to stay out of traps. Second, athletes must understand the mechanics of moving out of traps. Bearing this in mind, it's possible to cope with zone pressure defenses.

The Replacement Attack offers opportunity to move the ball up-court fast. One of the ideas of beating zone pressure is to pass the ball up rather than use the dribble excessively.

A danger point in the Replacement Attack against pressure is that zone presses fundamentally shift the zone to the ball side of the court, and in many cases they over-shift to the lane of the ball. This means that if the offense attacking the same lane of the ball and the zone is over-shifted to that lane, there are opportunities to intercept passes. Something a little different in strategy must be tried to put the pressure on the defense. This can be accomplished by moving to the opposite side of the court, taking advantage of the zone shifting and also of the open unguarded area.

An example of the attack on zone pressure is shown in Diagram 7-7. One passes the ball to 2, who passes to 4 down the right sideline.

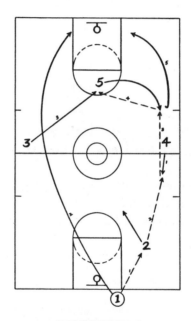

DIAGRAM 7-7
Replacement Attack Against Full-Court Zone Pressure

Four passes to 5 moving over from his zone pressure standard alignment to receive the pass, and 5 passes the ball to 3 moving toward the middle-court area. Meanwhile 1 has moved up-court to take the left wing position. Three is in the middle area, and 5 moves in to assume the right wing position.

One way to make the attack a little more efficient is to use quicker passes to the mid-court area.

It must be remembered that a player receiving a pass while moving to the ball should turn and face the basket in order to perceive up-court action and also look to pass ahead to continue the flow of the attack toward the basket. If a player moving to the ball cannot receive a pass, his job is to cut away from the ball and move to the far end of the court rather than chance the possibility of two defensive players guarding three offensive players. The players should keep spread out.

COACHING GUIDELINES

1. The players should use fakes when necessary to move into a position to receive the ball against all man-for-man defenses.
2. Sharp and crisp chest, baseball, or bounce passes should be available for ball movement.
3. When players receive a pass, they should look ahead immediately to examine the passing possibilities.
4. When balancing the floor with the balance wheel, remember the shooting, passing, and driving possibilities.
5. In the Replacement Attack against zones, move a big man back to the pivot position, if this is desired, by a simple exchange with a small man.
6. Attacking full-court man-to-man pressure, be aware of the possibility of moving the ball toward the basket with both passing and dribbling.
7. If the ball is moved to an offensive corner, be ready to pass to the pivot area or drive to the basket with minimum delay. A shot may also be in order if close to the basket.
8. In beating zone pressure, remember the principle of zones over shifting to the strong side. Consequently, be able to move the ball out of the danger area to the middle of the court or to the opposite side.

8

The Weak-Side
Crash Attack

The first two options focused the attack in the lane of the ball and one lane to either side. Remembering that the floor is divided into three lanes from baseline to baseline, option one originates in the middle lane, ending with scoring pressure from that lane. In option two, the attack is focused in a side lane with the ball brought to the middle for convergence on the basket. The third option, the Weak-Side Crash Attack, is geared and designed to batter at the opponent from the weak-side lane, which is two lanes removed from the location of the ball. For example, the ball may be controlled in the right lane in the initial movement, but the real intent is to clear a player in the left or weak-side lane, and then to give that player the ball by way of a pass to the middle lane, then another pass to the open player in the left lane.

If the cutting weak-side player is not clear, then there is follow-up action that sets up shots in close to the basket. The third option, as in all the rest, develops multiple shot opportunities off the four steps. The first opportunity takes place with a pass to the weak-side cutter, the second from the post position, and the third from a position by the original passer moving behind the post man. A slash then develops with player movement into the internal zone, followed by the balance wheel and the Weak-Side Crash if necessary.

Use of the blind or weak-side maneuver did not become popular until after 1950. Although used on occasions, it was to be exploited commencing from that time to the present. The objective of this play was to combat over-shifting defenses geared to stop movement between the ball and basket while forgetting about the players away from the ball. Most coaches realized that players off the ball had a definite place in the pattern other than just rebounding or moving to keep the defense honest. Strong-side action often is used with the real intent being to set up a variety of plays with the off-the-ball players. The sound offensive basketball systems bring the players to the ball, but they also include taking the ball to the players.

We include option three sporadically to take advantage of overbearing ball lane teams and to strike quickly during each game, although weak-siding is implemented and prolonged against full court pressure. The Weak-Side Crash is essentially a most important method in our system to defeat the presses when combined with the X Attack or the Replacement Attack. Between the three options, any evident defensive loopholes can be scrutinized with offensive pressuring. Zone press teams suffer the burden when coping with the Weak-Side Crash (Blind Pig, Back Door, or Back-Side Cut—as referred to by many coaches) due to the uncovered court area away from the ball. I incorporated the option into the system for extensive use against pressing zones after spending time at a clinic with Jack Ramsey—currently the coach of the Buffalo team in the National Basketball Association, and at that time head coach at St. Joseph's College in Philadelphia. Coach Ramsey was kind enough to privately elaborate on his techniques in beating pressure defenses. His whole pressure attack was founded on weak-side action. I incorporated many of his ideas into the Windsor attack, helping to make it much more effective.

Attacking Man-for-Man Defenses

The high post man is used when passing the ball to the weak side regardless of initial origin. The high post is necessary to clear the area around the deep internal zone for cutters. Long cross-court passes are made occasionally, but working off a man in the middle lane is more conducive to success. The method of attack with the basic cut against man-for-man is with the ball on one side of the court and the pivot man clearing the area by running to the side of the ball. The weak-side forward then moves in to the post for a pass. While this takes place, the weak-side guard makes a straight cut for the basket for a pass.

   An essential point may involve faking in order that a player may get free for a pass. Also of importance is that the post man takes the defender away far enough from the three-second area to make room for the cutter to move in unmolested. The weak-side forward coming into the post should try to force his man into an overplay situation and yet be positioned to receive a pass without deflection. Other players in the front-court area should be alert to race to the boards on a shot attempt to give offensive rebounding strength.

   Diagram 8-1 reveals the basis of the Weak-Side Crash. Two has the ball and waits for 5 to move to his lane, down deep toward the right

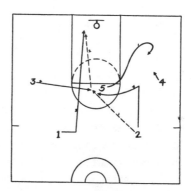

DIAGRAM 8-1
Weak-Side Crash Against Man-to-Man

corner. Three moves from the weak side to the high post area to receive a pass. One moves toward 2, and just as the ball is about to be released, 1 makes a sharp cut to the left and races directly to the basket for a pass from 5 and a lay-up shot. A pass at this point is better than a handoff.

   Continuing the action, if the cutter is not clear to receive a pass, 2 moves toward 4 as if to make an exchange, then cuts back behind 5 to take a jump shot. Five has the option of passing off to 2 for a jump shot or whirling around and driving toward the basket. Marty Kwiatkowski, a two-time All-Canadian player at Windsor University, was outstanding in the role of a forward on the Weak-Side Crash. Marty would move into the pivot from a weak-side position, and then after catching the pass he could make the split-second decision of passing the ball off or keeping it. He would then turn and face the basket, fake right or left to outwit his defensive man, and explode to the basket for a lay-up shot. He also could judge when to pass the ball off to a guard for the jumper. He was a fine player and a high scorer for three seasons after learning the maneuvers—including the jump shot from the free-throw area.

Diagram 8-2 shows slashing. When the post man cannot continue the offense, the slash takes place. In this case, 3 has the ball, and 5 sets

DIAGRAM 8-2
Weak-Side Crash Slash Against Man-to-Man

a screen for 4, who breaks off the screen and goes to the basket for a pass. If he is not clear, then 5 goes toward the basket and moves in for a potential shot. This gives an excellent inside threat with two big men underneath the basket in a favorable shooting area. It also gives a chance for big men to try hook shots and flip shots.

If no shot was taken and if 3, for example, has dribbled to the right side in a low post position as depicted in Diagram 8-3, after 4 and 5 have screened and rolled, then look for the balance wheel. Usually by this time the defense has sagged off trying to tie up 3. At this point we balance the floor with 3 passing off to 1 in the lower right corner, 2 moving to the upper right side even with the foul line, 4 moving to the upper left side, and 5 moving out to the lower left side. These movements form the perimeter set or balance wheel offense attack.

Diagram 8-4 shows another Weak-Side Slash possibility. Off the same set perimeter offense, 2 passes the ball to 1, who passes to 4. Four makes the pass to 5, who has worked an outside screen and reverse play with 3, while the ball was being passed. In this play, 3 puts an outside screen on 5's man, allowing 5 to step out behind the screen for a pass. The availability here is for a shot by 5 or a pass to 3

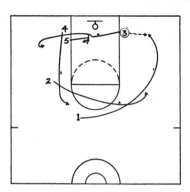

DIAGRAM 8-3
Balance Wheel from Weak-Side Crash

DIAGRAM 8-4
Weak-Side Slash Outside-Screen-and-Go

rolling underneath the basket, or a belated drive by 5 when 3 clears away from the basket. If nothing materializes, the balance wheel is still in effect and the ball can be passed around, probing for another weak-side slash.

Attacking Zone Defenses

In attacking all zones, the goal is to force the zone into the situation desired, and also to attack them with the various clocking movements. The weak-side slash option gets us into the zone alignment efficiently, while offering scoring opportunities on the cuts as well as on the individual phase of the attack.

Any zone offense must center around the threat of scoring off the pivot man. Zones try to cut off the middle, forcing the offense to move on the outside. Therefore, the middle may not open for the man to receive a pass. The guards may pass the ball back and forth once or twice, while the forwards try to set up at a post position. If this tactic proves unsuccessful, then the regular offense takes precedence. A point of importance is that a weak-side play is integrated into the regular pattern anyway through utilization of the center as the relay passer.

Diagram 8-5 illustrates the Weak-Side Crash initiating the zone attack. Two has the ball, 5 moves to the corner in one of the clock positions, 3 moves in to the post position, and 1 cuts to the basket. The scoring possibilities revolve around the pass to 3 into the post, since often on this type of movement he is clear for a quick jump shot at the foul line, as well as a pass inside to 1.

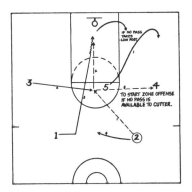

DIAGRAM 8-5
Weak-Side Crash Against Zones

The idea is to really make effective use of the man breaking into the area around the foul line or in the three-second lane, and with feet set to take a quick jump shot. Howard Sharpe, Head Coach at Gertsmeyer High School, Terre Haute, Indiana, discussed in a lecture at Adelphi University Basketball Clinic the merit of a player entering the scoring area ready to catch the pass and make a quick shot. Coach Sharpe had many fine ideas about the game of basketball. Like other great coaches, he emphasized the importance of little things in the game. In this instance, he said a player enters the lane with coordinated footwork, body and hands in position to shoot upon receiving the pass. Consequently, there is less chance for the shot to be blocked.

The regular zone offense takes place at this point, if the cutters are not clear. The point is that when 1 cuts to the basket—even against a zone—it is very possible that he may be clear for a short pass and a lay-up or a flip shot. One of the best scoring zone plays at Eastern High School was used often by a player named Frank Rowser. He seemed to find open shots inside the zone defense under the basket by simply moving through very slowly and making a sudden stop. Frank often received short passes from the post man for easy, close-in quick shots. As a result of observing Frank's tactics, and realizing their value, my teams added it to their system. It has been extremely successful for them through the years. The teams have been able to send a cutter slowly through the middle of the zone or near the middle of the zone with some change-of-pace movements to free himself to catch a pass.

The zone clocking movements take precedence at this particular point if there are no shots, and they continue until a desired shot is possible.

Attacking Full-Court Man-for-Man Pressure

Preparation for attacking the man-for-man is similar to all the other options, with the same rules in effect. The Weak-Side Crash works well when the full-court area is utilized. Often we spring a player loose with the ball just beyond mid-court all alone for a dribble to the basket. Tall defensive players once again are moved away from the basket area. In this particular case, guards and the more adept ball handlers usually receive the ball in areas where quick movement to the basket without being apprehended by any defensive tall men is possible. Of course, when tall men sag off to protect the area, it means that forwards and the center are probably clear for a short jump shot in close to the basket, so the offense serves its purpose very well.

Diagram 8-6 shows basic movement against full-court man-for-man pressure. One passes the ball to 2. Four clears out the side, moving near 5. Three moves to the middle for a pass from 2. One, who started his cut immediately after passing to 2, receives a pass down near the three-second lane for a move to the basket. Again 4 and 5 are in position to race to the board to rebound. Two is also in position to get a return pass from 3, while 3 may also bring the ball up-court with a possibility to score.

Diagram 8-7 shows another possibility off the Weak-Side Crash. It is similar to the first movement, except that in this case 2, after receiving the pass from 1, passes to 3 breaking in the middle. Four clears out to the right and 5 remains on the right side. One breaks

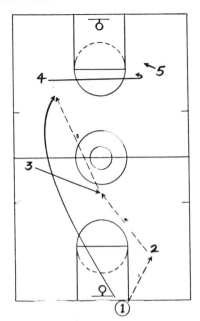

DIAGRAM 8-6
Initial Weak-Side Crash Against Full-Court Man-to-Man
Pressure

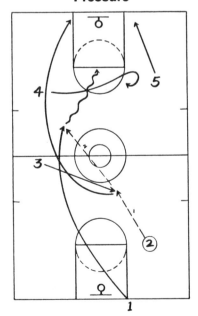

DIAGRAM 8-7
Alternate Weak-Side Crash Against Full-Court Man-to-Man
Pressure

toward the basket and receives the pass from 3, just after penetrating the offensive court. One dribbles the ball to the foul line and sets up the fast-break tandem with 3, who makes a break to the left wing, and 5, who goes to the right wing. Four doubles back to the trailer position, while 2 moves up slowly to a defensive position. This little additional rotation movement works well if 1 is aggressive in taking the ball to the lane and if 3 hustles to fill the left wing.

This play has been successful at Windsor, particularly when the team had Andy Auck, a versatile and alert 6'4" forward. Andy would pass the ball off to the cutter, then race for the basket to the left side open wing for a return pass and an easy lay-up.

Attacking Full-Court Zone Pressure

With the development of the Weak-Side Crash, teams have been able to successfully combat zone pressure defenses. Every zone offense has some method of forcing the pressure defense to over-shift to the ball and then to move the ball quicker than the players can move to the weak-side lane and up-court to a player in a shooting position. It was found that with this type of movement, the offense is extremely effective against almost any conceivable type of alignment. The Weak-Side Crash is probably the most effective weapon against zone pressure.

A team can use the Weak-Side Crash one or more times against zone pressure while bringing the ball up-court. The Crash may be used two or even three times in one continuous sequence when moving the ball up-court. Patience should be exercised to allow the defense to get out of position when utilizing planned moves and passing to the center area, then away from the defense. Most zone presses rotate to the ball; consequently, with proper tempo and alert playing, it is possible to move the ball to a man in the middle area and over to a weak-side player near the basket.

Diagram 8-8 shows the zone movement full-court. One passes the ball to 2, who passes the ball to 3 breaking to the middle from the left side. One moves away from his pass and up the left lane waiting for a pass from 3. Since the ball is well in the back court, 5 and 4 don't really have to move until 1 has the ball. Movement will take place in accordance to what 1 does with the ball. There are various ways of setting up the fast-break tandem, but the main factor here is that the ball remains away from the press and in the hands of an adept ball handler moving toward the basket.

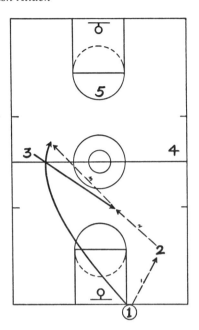

DIAGRAM 8-8
Weak-Side Crash in Back Court Against Full-Court Zone Pressure

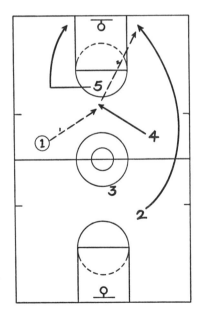

DIAGRAM 8-9
Weak-Side Crash in Front Court Against Full-Court Zone Pressure

An example of two weak-side plays is illustrated in Diagram 8-9 following the sequence of play and is correlated with Diagram 8-8, assuming that 1 receives a pass from 3 and is near mid-court, causing the zone pressure to shift left to stop the ball with a rotation flow toward the ball. There is a second Weak-Side Crash back to the right side court area. In Diagram 8-9, 1 sees that 5 clears out of the post to the left side; 4 moves from the right side to the post area and receives a pass from 1. Meanwhile, 2 moves up-court along the sidelines, breaks up the right lane to assume the wing position and is ready for a pass from 4 and a lay-up. Presumably, 1 is a back-court man and an excellent ball handler.

The Weak-Side Crash Attack gives a team enough movement to bring the ball up-court and also to set up highly organized shot attempts at the basket. If nothing develops with these attempts, then of course the object is to move into the regular offensive pattern in preparation to attack the standard drop-back defense of the opponent.

COACHING GUIDELINES

1. Timing of the weak-side cutter is important, as is the fake prior to his cut. He should be cutting about the same time the ball is passed to 5 and may use a change of pace on occasion to time his move.

2. When a weak-side crasher catches a pass while moving in for a shot, he must be alert to pass it off to a teammate under the basket when apprehended by a defensive player.

3. A weak-side crasher should always go to the corner on his side of the court rather than move to the opposite side. He should set up for a possible jump shot as close to the basket as his defensive man will allow.

4. The post man on the zone offense can come up as high as he needs to in order to receive a pass to start the attack rather than fight to stay at the foul-line area.

5. In using the Weak-Side Crash to defeat man-to-man pressure, the organization at the end of the attack should allow for free-lancing with the dribbler.

6. The important factor in attacking zone pressure is the attack conclusion. Defensive players will unite and congregate be-

tween the ball and the basket. Consequently, if there is no shot available immediately, the balance wheel may be set, or the regular offensive pattern may take place.

7. Zone pressure defenses overplay the lane of the ball; consequently, the Weak-Side Crash is an ideal attack.

9

The Center-Out Attack

The fourth option, or Center-Out Attack, uses the offensive abilities of the post man from a corner position. Located in a high post position where the play originates, the player moves out to a corner, receives a pass from a forward, then proceeds to return a pass to the cutter, jump shoot, or drive to the basket. We suffered the common dilemma of lacking a tall center at Windsor University. Many teams face the same problem. The Center-Out serves two main purposes against man-for-man defenses: (1) it forces a big opposing center to move out of the internal area to a corner to protect against a good shooting center, and (2) it permits a versatile offensive man to operate offensively against his opponent. In the first advantage, if the offensive center can shoot from the corner, it is possible to draw a big defensive center, intimidating offensive players in the internal zone out of that area. In the second advantage, the stress on versatility comes into play by permitting the offensive pivot man to use individual ability to out-maneuver his opponent. Quite often it is a different ball game when the intimidator must move to the outside to play defense due to slowness of foot, a lack of lateral movement, confusion, or any other reason. The diving player has the opportunity to use the hook shot, the flip shot, or the roll-back to offset his opponent.

Occasionally when a forward is in the post position, defensive teams guard him with a center. The forward may move out to the corner, drawing the big man out, then—permitting the regular offensive center to cut to the basket—double back to a low post to gain an ideal spot for a return pass, or simply to allow the forward to operate against the defender. Presumably the forward could outplay the bigger opponent. Gary Palano, an excellent mobile jump-shooting forward on two of Windsor's national championship teams, was excellent in the role of giant killer. Gary would start at the post position, then migrate to the corner and take the tall defender with him. After receiving the pass, Gary would let fly his excellent jump shot or would skirt around his man for an easy lay-up.

If the opposition permits the tall man to move out continually, then a slash with the regular post-man or one of the other big forwards into the pivot is available for internal shooting, often with a favorable mismatch in player size.

The cutter in this attack originates from a forward position after passing to the player in the corner. From this side position, the cutter moves to the basket for a return pass or doubles back to the low post on the same side. From either move he then sets up a slash with a screen on the other side of the basket, for the weak-side forward. The weak-side forward and cutter then executes a split-up-and-down play. Usually one of these two is open for the shot. If neither is, then clearing out permits the player with the ball in the corner to again have time to drive his opponent, the first drive situation occuring before the cut.

This simple option can be extremely useful. By using it early in the game to test out the reaction of the opponents in relation to covering the corner area, it helps analyze the opponent's corner coverage and ability of players covering. It then becomes possible to proceed with the necessary offensive options for more effectiveness. The attack may be used in various spots during the game, too, or as a change of pace for offensive plays. Of course, if the tactics exploit defensive abilities and the defensive adjustments are inadequate, then the option is continued until there are diminishing returns due to defensive adjustments.

Once again, rebounding opportunities are enhanced because of the movement of offensive players and by drawing the bigger player away from the backboard. Offensive men can outwit defensive players in motion more readily.

Attacking Man-for-Man Defenses

The basic attack against a man-to-man defense is shown in Dia-

DIAGRAM 9-1
Center-Out Attack Against Man-to-Man Defense

gram 9-1. The idea is to pass the ball to a forward, who in turn passes to the center in a corner, then cuts to the basket to receive a return pass or allow for the man in the corner to shoot or drive. In the diagram, 2 passes to 4, who passes to 5 in the corner after moving from the high post position. Four then cuts sharply to the basket for a return pass. If he doesn't receive one, he proceeds to move away from the ball. One and 2 exchange positions to keep the defense honest and 3 starts moving down toward the baseline and then slowly moves toward the three-second area. The shots available are by 5 in the corner or off a drive, 4 on the close-in shot, or in some cases 1 after an exchange of position with 2 if he is in close enough to the basket to take a quick jumper. Rebounding comes from the three players closest to the basket, who in this case would be the three front men.

   Any twist can be used very well at this point in the slash movement. However, since movement is with the big men up front, it is wise to keep them in that area on this attack. The split-up-down is executed here and is depicted in Diagram 9-2. A slash takes place with 4 screening for 3. Then the split-up-and-down takes place. Three moves down toward the basket for a pass and 4 blocks 3's man and moves up toward the foul line. This maneuver can be reversed with 3 going to the foul line and 4 going to the basket. The object of this split is to cause confusion among the two defensive men and allow for quick movements by the screener and slasher to the two positions for a quick pass and a close-in shot. If no shots are available up to this point, then the balance wheel is formed.

   Diagram 9-3 depicts the balance wheel. In this situation, 3 is at a

DIAGRAM 9-2
Center-Out Attack Slash Against Man-to-Man Defense

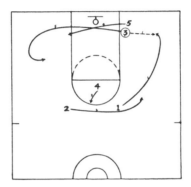

DIAGRAM 9-3
Balance Wheel from Center-Out

right low post with the ball and can't get a shot off. Five has moved across the basket to the weak side. One moves down to the low right side near the corner to start setting up the attack. Two fills the top right side, 4 moves up to fill the top left side post and 3, who passes the ball out to 1, moves out to the left side to fill the lower left spot. This forms the balance wheel along with 5 at the low post position on the left side.

From the balance wheel, 1 has the ball in the right corner as is shown in Diagram 9-4. One passes the ball to 2, who passes to 4, who passes to 3, and the offense is ready for a weak-side slash. In this particular slash, a pivot-clear-out is shown. In other words, 3 gets the ball and 5 clears out. Three dribbles into the basket on a drive. If he can't penetrate to shoot, he dribbles out to the left corner and looks for

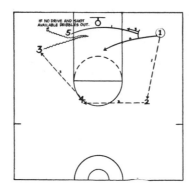

DIAGRAM 9-4
Weak-Side Slash Pivot-Clear-Out

1 to come across to the post position, helped by a screen from 5. Five rolls down low. This is similar to the high-low-split as in the slash. With these movements taking place off the weak-side slash, every player is in a shooting position as the desirable inside action takes place.

Attacking Zone Defenses

Cutting is similar in the zone attack as in the basic man-for-man attack. However, the flow starts in one direction but ends up going in the opposite. The option starts either to the right or left, even though the diagrams depict going to the right. Another point to remember is that the wave attack is always in effect. This means that the ball is passed to any player open for a shot prior to starting the clocking movement.

In Diagram 9-5, player 2 has the ball and passes to 4 at the forward position. Five moves down toward the basket and to the corner to receive a pass from 4. That is the Center-Out part of the option. Four passes to 5 and cuts through the lane, looking for a pass, and if he doesn't receive one he goes to the low post opposite the ball. Three crosses over to the low post on the side of the ball, and 1 and 2 exchange.

The follow-up for this initial play is shown in Diagram 9-6 with 5 in the corner possessing the ball. He starts the proper clocking movement. A problem here may arise since someone must play the pivot

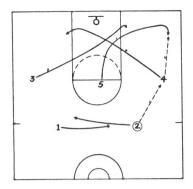

DIAGRAM 9-5
Center-Out Attack Against Zone

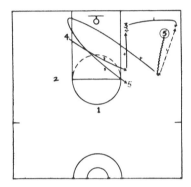

DIAGRAM 9-6
Center-Out Variation Against Zone

position. In this particular case, 4, after cutting through initially and moving away from the ball, doubles back and commands the post position. Five starts the proper movement by dribbling away from the corner and passing to 3, then cuts straight to the basket looking for the availability of being open. If he is not, 4 rolls down the lane for a pass or to assume that clocking low post offensive position, while 5 moves up to play the high post. This tactic gives some more internal zone movement while returning the center to his position if so desired. Now 3 is the player officially starting the clock movement. The zone offense is set with the positions properly filled, and all the maneuvers and rotations are available at this particular point.

Attacking Full-Court Man-to-Man Pressure

The Center-Out Attack works quite well against the man-to-man pressure defenses, too. The movement once again is identical with the center cutting to the basket. It takes place on the larger area of the court and there is more movement to get to the basket area. The object is to set up the fast-break tandem near the basket. Diagram 9-7 shows the

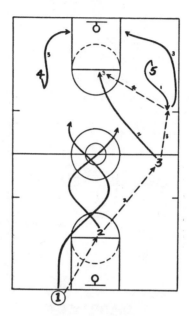

DIAGRAM 9-7
Initial Center-Out Attack Against Full-Court
Man-to-Man Pressure

basic attack against man-to-man pressure. One passes the ball to 2, who passes to 3, at mid-court. As 5 moves toward the basket, then comes up to a position on the right side to receive a pass from 3, player 3 could dribble first, then pass, or pass directly to 5. At this point the attack resembles the replacement, option three, except that 3 makes the pass to 5 and breaks full speed to stop at the high post position. Four takes the left wing position, and the tandem that is set up is between 5, 4, and 3. Meanwhile, 1 and 2 reverse either once or twice while coming up-court with the player most accessible as the trailer.

Here is another variation of this same actual tandem setup but bringing the guard up-court on the side of the tandem. In this particular play, shown in Diagram 9-8, most of the movements are identical,

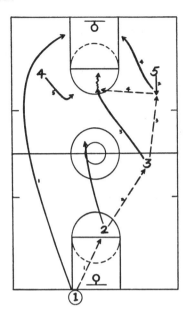

DIAGRAM 9-8
Center-Out Alternate Against Full-Court Man-to-Man Pressure

with 1 passing the ball to 2, who passes to 3. Three passes to 5 who passes to 3, cutting toward the foul line, and then 5 reverses and moves into form the right wing of the tandem. One, at this point, races full-court to set up the tandem by taking a left wing position. Two moves up gradually, and in this particular play 4 is a key figure because he moves out, then back into a trailer position ready to attack from there. These movements open up opportunities for scoring thrusts from various areas of the court and set up the well-organized tandem at the end with the necessary four players.

Attacking Zone Pressure Defenses

A Center-Out Attack against zone pressure also has the characteristics of the replacement but ends up with the difference being the cut of one of the passers to the basket or to a wing position. Of course, the purpose is to catch the press overshifting to the strong side as well as offensively being able to go inside the press, then attack the back men on the press before the other defensive members can move back to protect. Passing the ball rather than dribbling exploits the philosophy of attack and shooting within five seconds after throwing the ball inbounds. Once again, however, caution must be taken not to force passes after the initial thrust. At this time the player with the ball must realize the danger imposed by the zone retreat. The ball must be controlled with a player in charge to restart the option.

Diagram 9-9 shows the movements against zone presses—1 throwing to 2 and moving up-court. Two passes to 4, then cuts full speed toward the basket. Four passes the ball to 5, who moves to the high forward position. Four cuts to the strong-side wing position. Three comes in on the weak-side wing position, while 5 passes to 2 in the center court area, establishing a tandem. Five is the trailer.

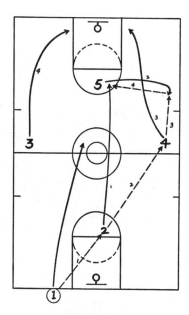

DIAGRAM 9-9
Center-Out Attack Against Full-Court Zone Press

COACHING GUIDELINES

1. Use the Center-Out option to draw a big man away from the backboard. The offensive center should stay as close to the basket as the defense allows him to in order to be a jump-shooting threat.
2. Guards should reverse to keep the defense honest.
3. Be ready to take advantage of pivot men who have difficulty guarding a man out in a corner.

4. On the split-up-and-down play, be ready to have the player in the corner with the ball ready to take advantage of the open man. Usually this opening may only be for a movement.

5. When cutting through on zones, always look for the passing availability.

10

The 3-on-3 Option
in the Cut-and-Slash Attack

The 3-on-3 Attack is the fifth option. This attack was installed in recent years to take further advantage of the versatile development of Windsor's front line. Eddie Chittaro, the Assistant Coach at Windsor University, and I decided that if the players worked so diligently to develop as total ball players and since the inside-out-type of scoring was a factor in winning basketball games, it would be practical to take advantage of the three front players' abilities to put sound basketball principles of offense into effect. Six plays were designed to be used, involving only the pivot man and forwards. Each play is started by the pivot man. This attack originates off the pivot man in the center lane, with the guards primarily reversing to exchange positions with each other, keeping their defensive men away from the play action. While the Center-Out option is developed primarily between the three front-line men too, it originates off the forwards, and only uses a basic cut and slash. However, the 3-on-3 option is really three-on-three basketball between the three front-line players against their defenders.

At the time of inception, Eddie and the writer were influenced by the philosophy of small players often scoring off the fast break with the tall players scoring more off the set patterns. In each case players were attacking from the internal zone, only under different conditions, with emphasis placed upon the different mode of attack. The other influential point was that since versatility was stressed and development of this type of play was successful—especially with the larger players—it would be practical to use this development to serve a distinct advantage, particularly if the opposition had a player lacking in defensive versatility and a player with definite defensive weaknesses. In other words, the team tried to use its versatility to exploit players with vulnerable defensive abilities. Although many plays were tried at first, six were discovered that are currently most expedient and useful.

The fifth option, the 3-on-3 Attack, is used often to challenge teams with big players particularly using man-for-man defense. It is tried each game, and it may be used effectively against zone defenses as well as against full-court pressure defenses. It is used extensively against man-for-man sagging teams. Sagging defenses are forced deep into the internal zone, opening the chance to shoot within six to eight feet of the basket whenever lay-ups are not available in the initial thrust.

Once again rebounding advantage is a chief ingredient in the attack because of the movement favoring the offensive team. It is easier to rebound when forcing the defensive players to fight through screens, to move often, and to attempt to block shots in close to the basket by often jumping up and leaving the ground. The Windsor team's players enjoy rebounding. Joe Bardswitch, a 6'4" center for two seasons, didn't have any exceptional spring or leaping ability, but with quick moves and aggressiveness he became an outstanding rebounder for both seasons. He took delight in outrebounding his taller opponents on the offensive boards while scoring many points for Windsor University.

Attacking Man-for-Man Defenses

The high post alignment is utilized in the fifth option. It is started with a pass to a post man. Prior to commencing the attack, there is movement on the part of the forwards—as well as the post man—to secure offensive position and alignment. Ideally the post man stations himself just outside the foul-line area, but it is not imperative that he stay in that spot. He has freedom to move around within the free-throw circle. The *forwards' flat-cut* is the first play, and it is combined with the second play or the center-follow-up if no shot is available off the former. The forwards' flat-cut is shown in Diagram 10-1. Two passes the ball to a high post man; then 2 and 1 exchange positions. As this takes place, 4 moves up toward the center court and makes a flat-cut to

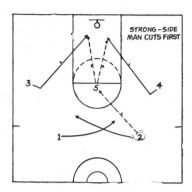

DIAGRAM 10-1
3-on-3 Attack Forward's Flat-Cut Against Man-to-Man Defense

the basket. Four makes the first flat-cut because he is the right forward and the ball was passed in from 2 on the right strong side. As soon as it is apparent that 4 can't get loose, 3, the weak-side forward, flat-cuts to take the shot. Meanwhile, if neither is clear, they exchange sides and take a wing position on either side of the basket in good shooting areas. It must be explained that the initial flat-cut by 4 finds him crossing over to the left side very rapidly to make room for 3 to flat-cut and avoid congesting the three-second area. There also exists the possibility of 4 flat-cutting, and when he realizes there is no chance to fool the defensive man, he may move to the right side of the court temporarily, wait for 3 to flat-cut, and then exchange positions with 3 if there is no pass made.

In Diagram 10-2 the *center-follow-up* is seen after the two flat-cuts. This has been an excellent play for Windsor through the years. Tim Henderson, a fine 6'5" post man on two national championship Windsor University teams, executed this play to perfection. He would make the pass to either wingman, with excellent judgment as to how far to take his man toward the basket before changing directions and going behind the post man for a pass. This move, along with his excellent jump shot, helped the team over many rough spots during the season. In Diagram 10-2, 5 passes to 3, then breaks toward the basket, cuts to the right moving behind 3 for the jump shot. One and 2 exchange and if they find themselves standing too long, they should exchange again.

The third play with the 3-on-3 is the *center-forward screen-and-roll,* shown in Diagram 10-3. In this play, 2 passes to 5 as player 4

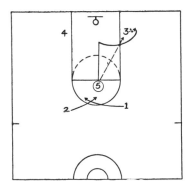

DIAGRAM 10-2
3-on-3 Attack Center-Follow-Up Against Man-to-Man Defense

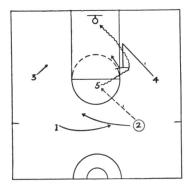

DIAGRAM 10-3
3-on-3 Attack Center-Forward Screen-and-Roll
Against Man-to-Man Defense

begins to flat-cut, then returns to screen just outside the three-second area. Five drives off the screen to the outside. By going to the outside of the screen the play is more effective, since it gives the opportunity for 5 to stop and jump shoot right at that spot, with less opposition from the defensive player guarding 4. Five also may have less opposition when driving to the basket. Four also has a better angle to receive a pass on a roll-in move. Meanwhile, 3 moves in for a rebound while 1 and 2 exchange positions.

In Diagram 10-4, we see the fourth possibility, the *forward-screen-and-go*. Once again 2 passes to 5, who dribbles off the screen set by 4; but instead of moving to the basket, he dribbles toward the corner and stops. Four proceeds laterally across the three-second lane

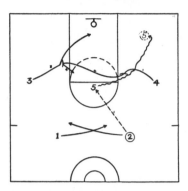

DIAGRAM 10-4
3-on-3 Attack Forward-Screen-and-Roll
Against Man-to-Man Defense

and sets a screen on the weak-side for 3. Four and 3 have high-low-split. If 3 goes low, then 4 comes back high; if 3 comes high toward the foul line, then 4 goes low. Five then passes to the man available. Player 5 may also take a short jump shot, since the other players, 3 and 4, are in excellent rebounding positions. Meanwhile 1 and 2 exchange positions.

The *outside-forward screen play* is the fifth and is executed as depicted in Diagram 10-5. Two passes to 5 who turns toward the basket. Meanwhile 1 and 2 are exchanging. Four moves from the right

DIAGRAM 10-5
3-on-3 Attack Outside-Forward Screen
Against Man-to-Man Defense

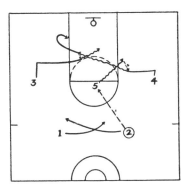

DIAGRAM 10-6
3-on-3 Attack Weave Against Man-to-Man Defense

side behind 3, who sets an outside screen just to the left of the three-second area midway between the foul line and the basket. Five passes to 4 for a shot. Four may pass to 3, who cuts to the basket. Meanwhile, 5 moves in for the rebound.

The *weave,* the sixth and final play, is shown in Diagram 10-6. The weave in close to the basket may be extremely effective because of the possibility of a short jump shot against a sagging defense. A hand-off and cut-in toward the basket is also possible. In the diagram, 2 passes to 5. Five dribbles to the right and hands off to 4. Five then moves toward the basket. Four dribbles left and hands off to 3, moving right. Four rolls to the basket and into position to continue the weave if no shots were taken. Often one of the best plays off the weave is to fake a handoff and suddenly drive to the basket for a lay-up. The shots available off the 3-on-3 are lay-ups, in some cases hook shots, and also short jump shots.

The balance wheel is formed in Diagram 10-7 by having 5, who is near the basket with the ball and can't shoot, pass to 1 breaking to the right corner. Two is in the right top position, 3 assumes the top left position, and 4 crosses the court to the lower left position. Five is inside at the left low post position, and the wheel has been formed.

The balance wheel may be formed in conjunction with any of the six plays whenever needed. The same is true of the weak-side slash plays which may always originate after the balance wheel formation.

In Diagram 10-8, another one of the weak-side slash plays is shown. In this particular play, 1 has the ball and passes to 2, who in turn passes to 3. Player 3 passes to 4, and then 3 moves opposite the pass and screens for 2. Then 2 moves to the basket in a position to

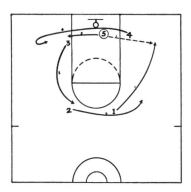

DIAGRAM 10-7
Balance Wheel from 3-on-3

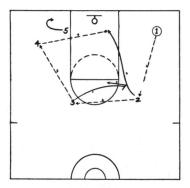

DIAGRAM 10-8
Weak-Side Slash Screen Opposite Play

receive a pass from 4 for a shot. Three also moves toward the free-throw line for a pass and a possible shot. Five moves away from the ball toward the left corner to open up the three-second or to receive a pass from either cutter 2 in case there is no shot available. If he receives a pass, 5 can jump shoot. If the shot is taken by 2 or 3, then he can serve as a rebounder.

Attacking Zone Defenses

The 3-on-3 can be used against zone defenses, too. The idea behind the movement is to cut the forwards through the three-second lane looking for an easy basket. If this does not take place, it is relatively simple to proceed into the clock offense. The post man is

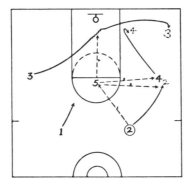

DIAGRAM 10-9
3-on-3 Attack Against Zones

DIAGRAM 10-10
3-on-3 Attack Pivot Sudden-Move Against Zones

already in position. Consequently, the offense needs very little time to set up.

In Diagram 10-9, 2 passes to 5 and moves to the right forward spot. Three moves through the center area from the left and moves into the clocking lower right corner position. Four follows this move by going to the basket and cutting back to the low right post in the clocking position, and 1 moves to the weak-side position. In the diagram, 2 passes to 5. Five can pass to cutter 3 or 4, and if this is not available, 5 can pass the ball out to 2, who is in position either to shoot or to pass the ball to 3 to begin the regular zone offense.

Occasionally a sudden move by the pivot man toward the basket can catch a lackadaisical defense off balance, permitting him a lay-up shot. In Diagram 10-10, 2 passes to 5. Five passes to 4, who passes to

3 in a lower right-hand clocking position. Five fakes a move toward the basket and moves up to the foul line, then suddenly pivots and cuts to receive a pass from 3 for a lay-up shot. The cardinal rule is to keep the defensive team off balance by looking for key movements to pick up two cheap points, which in crucial situations may demoralize the opponent. Along with this, it also puts a little more pressure on the defense and opens up more potential scoring from the regular zone offense.

Attacking Man-for-Man Pressure Defenses

A 3-on-3 Attack can be used quite effectively against man-to-man presses, as can all of the options, if it is used correctly. In the full-court press attack, the first thing is to move the ball inbounds and then pass it ahead to the three big men, who through their passing and cutting will develop scoring opportunities. The three players do not necessarily use the six plays while the ball is being brought up court. Instead, the three players try to set up a fast-break tandem between themselves. If a quick thrust is not possible, however, and the ball is brought over mid-court with the three players in normal alignment, then any of the six plays takes precedent.

In Diagram 10-11, an example of the 3-on-3 offense against the man-to-man full-court press can be seen. One passes inbounds to 2, then 2 passes ahead to 3 coming into the middle area from the left side. Three turns toward the basket to make a pass to 5 and then cuts full speed to the basket, outracing his man to receive a pass from 5 for the lay-up. Four goes to the foul line. Meanwhile, 2 moves up court to take the trailer position. Once again, the reader will notice the forming of a fast-break front with three attackers and a trailer ready to descend upon the basket. The tandem can be used if 3 isn't clear. Five would pass to 4, who would start a tandem play.

Attacking Zone Pressure Defenses

Attacking zone pressure may be possible with the 3-on-3 with the object being to organize with a fast-break tandem at the end of the attack. Diagram 10-12 shows a pass from 1 to 2. Two passes to 3, who passes to 5 on the left wing and then moves up to take the foul-line position with 4 on the right side forming a tandem by moving up to the right wing position. Two moves up court and gets into the trailer

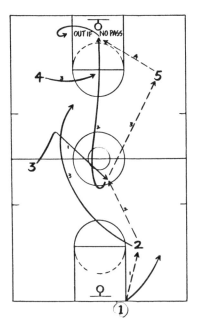

DIAGRAM 10-11
3-on-3 Attack Against Full-Court Man-to-Man Press

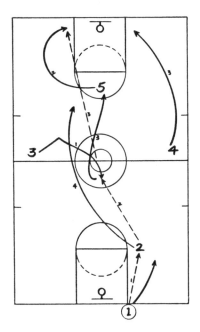

DIAGRAM 10-12
3-on-3 Attack Against Full-Court Zone Press

position. The value of the 3-on-3 against a zone press is that a pass to 3 in the middle court area enables him to pass to either side against a zone.

The zone will usually try to utilize the second trapping principle: two men on the ball, two floaters and one safety man. This allows passes to the strong or weak side against this principle, and it is a good way to start an organized movement to the basket. If nothing develops in the full-court attack, then the balance wheel can be formed or the players can move to the regular offensive alignment and attack the basic defense with a 3-on-3 option.

COACHING GUIDELINES

1. Players should use fakes and reverses to keep the defensive man from standing in a stationary position.
2. When flat-cutting against man-to-man defenses, designate the player on the strong side to be the first cutter. On occasion it may be advisable to change and have the man on the weak side be the first cutter.
3. After the guards exchange positions, with the pattern play still in process, they should exchange positions again and keep moving closer in toward the foul line to be shooting threats.
4. A big man may play any of the three front positions for the 3-on-3 Attack.
5. Big men must be responsible for rebounding positions, since the guards stay back near the foul line.
6. Be alert on the weave to make a cut up the middle for a pass and an easy shot at the basket.
7. If the weak-side slash doesn't work at first, pass the ball around, scanning the defense to attempt another individual balance wheel play, then try another weak-side slash if necessary.

11

The Rub-Off Attack

Earlier in the text, it was mentioned that the Cut-and-Slash included most facets of modern basketball. The attack includes offensive theories that ingenious coaches teach evolving from basic principles of modern offensive basketball. These principles build the foundation to offensive movement for effective scoring. For example, three such principles are the criss-crossing offenses, the pass and cut offenses, and the rub-off offenses. Each coach develops a system appropriate to his philosophy of the game. The coach must make many decisions as to the type of offensive principles to use and must be flexible to change if the system has breakdowns.

Some offenses are geared around individual moves like the give-and-go, or movement with three players, as in the weave attack. Along with the basic movement of an offense are included many individual movements or drives and a combination of various principles of individual play. I have discussed nearly all the basic offenses and individual plays in basketball because of the versatility of our attack. We use these various maneuvers because of the importance for an outstanding offensive team to include them in its repertoire of plays. There has been one type of attack not discussed yet, to be analyzed at this time. The attack referred to is the sixth and final option, the Rub-Off Attack. This offense borrows from the theory of the Shuffle Offense. Although we have outlined the rub-off type of individual movements in the other options, none has included the initial movement of this type. The other options dealt mainly with the first move as a cutter movement. This option contrastingly starts with a slasher-type movement originating from a player away from the ball rather than the passer.

In this sixth option, emphasis is placed upon a style resembling the Shuffle Offense. The Shuffle Offense was brought back to the game of basketball as an outstanding offensive weapon by Coach Joel Eaves of the University of Auburn in Auburn, Alabama, to attack the man-for-man defenses primarily. Coach Eaves did a masterful job of streamlining the Shuffle Offense. The attack had an impact on basketball that brought back a whole new dimension to offensive aspects of the game. Many basketball coaches throughout the country on all levels of play, including high schools and colleges, adopted the Shuffle Attack practically in its entirety. Others used the basics of what Coach Eaves called the Third Option. My teams borrowed some movements from the Shuffle Offense, and particularly the basic philosophy of the Third Option, and called it the Rub-Off Offensive Attack.

The term *rub-off* is used to describe a screen play out beyond the free-throw line and off the post man. This is different from the screen and split-in-and-out play which has its inception from the side of the three-second lane. It is easier to distinguish between the two when referring to them in that context.

Initially, the Rub-Off Attack is started with a pass from one guard to the other, followed by a pass to the forward. During this passing sequence, the first guard cuts for the basket after executing a series of fakes, followed by the second guard after he too executes a series of fakes. If no scoring opportunities are present, the next three sequential steps, as outlined in all basic options, take place.

A unique feature of this option is the simplicity in repeating the first step of the attack on a continuity basis. For example, the offense may begin with the rub-off cuts by passing the ball to one forward. Then the players exchange positions and pass the ball to the opposite forward, rub off again with the opposite movements and actually have a continuity of movements with the initial step of the attack, until ready to start the second, or slashing, step of the offense. This tactic makes the Rub-Off Attack extremely useful because it offers the benefits of continuity, eventually releasing cutters for lay-ups. The nature of the movements and the continuity can deceive the defense, as the defense anticipates the regular pattern sequence. Control of game tempo against man-for-man defenses is also possible.

The cutting movement actually differs from the third option of the Shuffle in that it is a four-player movement rather than a five-player movement, as taught by Coach Eaves during his tenure. The player at the high post position remains stationary instead of exchanging his position.

Coach Ted Kjolhede, the former mentor at Central Michigan University and currently Athletic Director at that school, was extremely successful developing outstanding teams using the four-man shuffle rather than the conventional five. The initial movement in the rub-off is similar to that designed by Coach Kjolhede.

The Rub-Off Attack is similar in alignment to all of the other options, and is of course a high post attack. It may be used against any type of defense, with some minor adjustments that will be explained in the discussion of attacking zones as well as attacking the pressure defenses. It is exceptionally effective against the man-for-man defense, and it is implemented for long periods in many games.

An outstanding feature of the attack deals with the excellent shot possibilities that could develop. This type of movement opens the way to afford lay-ups to the cutters, a move-in by the post man for close-to-the-basket shots, and short jump shots from the outside positions. A second feature is the inclusion of excellent rebounding position as in the other options. With these factors in mind, we are ready to describe the attack.

Attacking Man-for-Man Defenses

The initial alignment and rub-off movement is shown in Diagram 11-1. One passes the ball to 2, who passes to 4. Meanwhile, 1 makes a

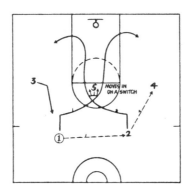

DIAGRAM 11-1
Rub-Off Attack Against Man-to-Man Defense

series of fakes, then breaks off 5 to the basket. If he does not receive a pass, he proceeds to the right side of the court. Two follows the same procedure except that he moves to the left side of the court after 1 cuts. Three waits for 2 to cut, fakes a cut-in, then moves out for a jump shot in a position on the short left side. Five looks for a move-in if his defensive man leaves him on a switch situation, which could leave him facing the basket with the cutter's defensive man behind 5, making it possible for 5 to receive a pass for a close-in shot.

At this point, it would be very simple to add the continuity phase to the first step by passing the ball around the perimeter to the other side of the court and making similar cuts. Diagram 11-2 shows the

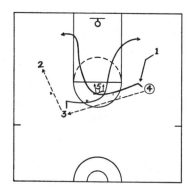

DIAGRAM 11-2
Rub-Off Cutting Step Continuity Against Man-to-Man Defense

continuity phase. Four passes the ball to 3, who passes to 2, while 4 fakes and breaks off 5, then 3 breaks off 5 after faking, and 1 fakes toward the lane and moves off to the right side for a jumper. Actually, it is more effective to alternate between the step attack and continuity when using the Rub-Off Attack over a long period of time in a game.

The slashing attack, when needed, takes place after the initial attack and is shown in Diagram 11-3. Assuming that the initial move was run with no continuity, the players proceed with the attack from new positions. Four has the ball, while 5 moves from his post position to set a screen of the side of the lane for 3. Three moves off the screen for a high-low-split. In this instance, 3 moves to the high position and 5 rolls low towards the basket. Player 4 has the option of passing to either man who is open, with the first possibility developing with 3 shooting a jumper, the second possibility with 5 shooting a lay-up.

DIAGRAM 11-3
Rub-Off Attack Slash Against Man-to-Man Defense

Player 3 could move low off the screen and 5 could move high. If this happened, 3 would be the first available receiver and 5 the second. Either the lay-up by 3, or a short jumper by 5 at the free-throw line is possible. Meanwhile, 1 and 2 return to the defensive positions. Rebounding is done by the player splitting and not shooting and also player 4.

When the slash attack terminates and nothing has materialized, then the movement is to the balance wheel. This is accomplished by balancing the floor with players as in the other options. Diagram 11-4 shows the movement to the balance wheel. Assuming that 3 has the ball at the free-throw line with no available shot, then he passes right to 1 in the top right spot, while 4 fills in the low right spot. Two takes in

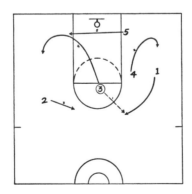

DIAGRAM 11-4
Balance Wheel from Rub-Off

the top left spot, and 3 moves to the low left spot after passing to 1. Five remains inside at the low left post position. Formation of the balance wheel can be initiated from the free-throw line or even out further if necessary. From the balance-wheel offense, a player may make an individual drive or take a jump shot; otherwise the ball is passed around the perimeter to initiate the weak-side slash.

The weak-side slash play is depicted in this instance as the double-screen, even though all of the other slashes described in the previous options could be used. Diagram 11-5 shows the double-

DIAGRAM 11-5
Rub-Off Weak-Side Slash Double-Screen Play

screen. One passes the ball to 2, while 3 and 5 set up a double screen along the left side of the three-second lane. Four moves along the baseline and sets himself up behind the double screen to receive a pass from 2 for a jump shot behind the double screen. If either defensive player's man guarding 5 or 2 tries to block the shot attempt, then 1 looks to pass the ball to the offensive player left unguarded and move to the basket. The double-screen is especially effective against the sagging element of a man-for-man defense. A shot may be taken by 2 if the defense sags too far in toward the basket. If the weak-side slash doesn't work, the balance wheel can be set up again and the double-screen can be tried again, or another one of the weak-side plays can be developed.

Attacking Zone Defenses

Probably the first element a coach would question concerning the implementation of the Rub-Off Attack against a zone defense would be the feasibility of the offense against the defensive zone type of movements and coverage. The rub-off type of cuts do not serve any purpose against the defenses that guard areas of the court rather than a specific assignment of one player staying with another. An offensive man can rub his defensive counterpart off on another offensive player if he tries to follow him at all times. The defensive players in a zone only guard floor areas with some man-for-man responsibilities if there is an offensive player in that area.

Of course, a coach could be correct in commenting about the uselessness of a rub-off. Generally speaking, there is no merit in this type of rub-off move, since the front men on defense would not penetrate deeply enough into the lane to be blocked out by a rub-off. However, the rub-off type of movement minus the blocking action by the post man can be useful in setting up the regular zone offense. The two guards can move into the offense just by cutting to the basket with the off-the-ball criss-cross tactics. It would give a fluid flow of players into the zone attack, while it offers the possibility of a cutter moving into the lane to receive a pass for a shot.

The rub-off basic cut movement against zones is shown in Diagram 11-6. One passes to 2, who passes to 4. Meanwhile, 1 cuts to the basket to the right of the post man, followed by 2 cutting the opposite side of the post man with no faking to the basket. Both look for close-in shots in sequence, then leave the lane area if none is available. Player 1 ends up in the corner offensive position on the right side, and 3 takes the right low post position, while 2 doubles back to fill the top position on the left side. Actually, 3 can be considered a cutter also,

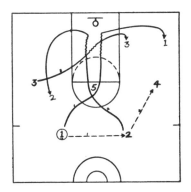

DIAGRAM 11-6
Rub-Off Attack Against Zones

since he moved inside the three-second lane in his advance to the right low post position. If no shot has been made available even after all of these individual moves, then the clock offense is set up and the regular zone attack commences.

Attacking Full-Court Man-for-Man Pressure

The Rub-Off Attack can be used against man-for-man full-court pressure defenses with the same potential results as displayed against the man-for-man defense. Of course, the attack would take place over the full court. But there is merit to rubbing off players even far away from the basket. The benefit of this type of attack is usually derived by springing loose better ball handlers to receive a pass and penetrate to the basket. If nothing happens on the initial cutting phase, there are other movements possible, since there is still a lot of court area available. A clever offensive man could elude a defensive man more easily than would be possible in a more compact area.

In Diagram 11-7, the Rub-Off Attack full court is shown. Player 1 passes the ball to 2, who passes to 5 on the side. Meanwhile, 3 moves to the middle of the court and just over the ten-second line, to serve as

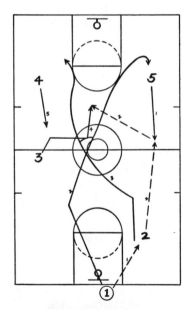

DIAGRAM 11-7
Rub-Off Attack Against Full-Court Man-to-Man Pressure

a screener. (It is important that 3 not set up on the ten-second line but to either side, and preferably in the front court.) In the diagram, 3 sets himself up just inside the ten-second line and screens for the first cutter, 1, moving from left to right. Two moves from the right side to the left side after 1 cuts. If there are no passes available, then 3 can move toward the basket to become the middle offensive man—in excellent position for a fast-break alignment, as is shown in the diagram. Three receives the pass from 5 and forms a fast-break tandem with 2 on the left wing and 1 on the right wing. Five would be the trailer and 4 would stay back on defense. Consequently, this movement offers opportunity for both cutters and the post man to receive passes and go for the basket. Another dimension is introduced whenever the offense starts far away from the basket. The players could repeat the movements as they progress closer to the basket. The second time around, the play would originate in almost the perfect starting point against the regular man-for-man defense. It is evident that a shuffle continuity offense against man-for-man full-court pressure could be very useful and practical, with a smooth transition into the next three steps if needed. Usually, against pressure, the offensive strike takes place with a quick thrust without excessive use of the continuity or the other three steps.

Attacking Full-Court Zone Pressure

The implication of the zone full-court pressure attack is that the cutters do not look for rub-offs against the post man but proceed to set up a secondary attack. Once the ball has been passed up court, then a fast-break alignment is set up. It is desirable to pass the ball rather than to dribble it toward the basket. The passing can offset pressing zone goals in which players are seeking to trap an offensive man with two defensive players. Occasionally it may be feasible to dribble against the zone to create advantages to pass while continuing the offense.

The attack against zone pressure is shown in Diagram 11-8. Player 1 inbounds the ball to 2, who passes the ball to 4. Meanwhile 1 and 2 criss-cross off 5. Notice that 1 ends up in the front court on the right side and 2 ends up at the point position near the free-throw circle. The reason for this is to beat the intended methods of the zone with quick passing. If 5 moved back to take the middle, the delay could allow the press to double up on 4 before this could be accomplished. So with 2 in the middle, 3 fills in the far lane on the left side for a

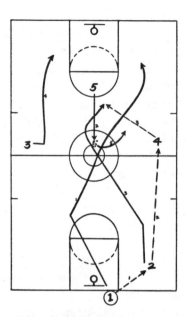

DIAGRAM 11-8
Initial Rub-Off Attack Against Full-Court Zone Pressure

fast-break tandem. Five would be the trailer and 4 the defensive safety man.

A variation of this play is shown in Diagram 11-9, where everything is the same—with one exception. In this diagram, 5 assumes the left wing to form the tandem as 3 moves toward the middle for an outlet pass, or to act as the trailer.

With these attacks the Rub-Off can combat any type of zone pressure defense with all the necessary ingredients. First, the ball is moved up court, then the fast-break alignment opens up avenues to score. It must be remembered that this pressure attack, like all the others, is set up in a regular zone pressure attack alignment just prior to commencing.

If an offensive player is trapped, his teammates must cope with the situation in accordance with the standard rules for escaping from any of the basic three traps. Caution must be taken when attacking, if unable to penetrate quickly for a score. Be alert to the fact that the defensive players will all rush to jam up the middle between the ball and the basket, and may intercept forced or careless passes in the three-second lane area.

This is a crucial time in the pressure zone attack since nearly 50

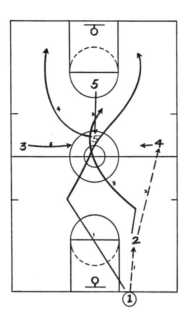

DIAGRAM 11-9
Rub-Off Attack Variation Against Full-Court Zone Pressure

percent of the steals, interceptions, and violations occur at this point. I recently made a brief study to ascertain when Windsor University's pressing defenses caused the opponents to make the most mistakes. It was found to his amazement that about 48 percent of the opponents' mistakes were made deep in our defensive area near the basket. The opponents either rushed the shot or passed carelessly laterally or backwards without any perception of our defensive players retreating to a position between the ball and the basket. The implications of this study forced us to adopt a policy of looking for another dimension of scoring when the zone attack bogged down. This dimension will be explained in the next chapter in the utilization of the Transitional Free-Lance Scoring Attack.

COACHING GUIDELINES

1. Timing is essential by the back court men on the initial cut. Use of fakes and changes of pace can be extremely helpful in hooking up the defensive man on the screener.
2. The forward receiving a pass should be prepared to pass

quickly to an open cutter. Look for the cutters in sequence first, then the post-man rolling down.

3. Both cutters should make themselves a scoring threat when in the three-second lane, rather than just running through the cut for the sake of motion.

4. The post man is generally the scoring threat in this initial cut, since he has two chances to block out a defensive man and create a switching situation, allowing him to be inside his new defensive man, with room in which to maneuver to the basket.

5. The continuity with the initial cut may be used for variety, increasing potential scoring effectiveness.

6. There is no need to rub a defensive man off on a post man against zone defenses or pressure zone defenses, but the pattern should be identical without fakes or rub-offs.

7. Against man-for-man full-court pressure, the rub-off may be repeated two or three times before springing a player loose for a lay-up shot, or setting up a fast-break alignment.

8. Passes should be quick and concise to avoid interceptions at all times, but particularly against the pressure defenses.

9. Be on the alert to help a player trapped by a zone press. A short outlet pass is usually the most effective release.

12

Transitional Free-Lance Scoring in the Cut-and-Slash

Most teams generally use two phases of attack in offensive basketball immediately after gaining possession of the ball. One phase is the fast break, which develops into many maneuvers in rapid-fire action that eventually lead into an outnumbering of the defensive players near the basket and a shot attempt. The other phase is the pattern offense, which takes place after the team cannot convert the fast-break attack into a score. The offensive team then waits for a team floor leader to take charge of the situation and waits for the pattern alignment to be established and to begin a formal pattern attack.

The elements of both phases include methods of securing ball possession, as in defensive rebounding of missed field goal attempts; rebounding of missed free-throw attempts; taking the ball after an opponent's successful basket, after his successful free throw, after a violation by the adversary or after being awarded the ball on a turnover—such as a steal or an interception. These elements make it possible for a team to gain control of the basketball and must be accounted for in planning offensive basketball. Ball possession may take place by exchanging ball control from the defensive team to the offensive team. Each phase makes it possible to set up scoring possibilities. One other method to be brought in here is the jump-ball play. On this play, the team securing the ball may fast-break or take time to develop an offensive set pattern.

There is a third phase implemented in an element of time that occurs between the other two phases that has not formally been exploited by many teams anywhere. This time element occurs from the moment the fast break ends—either in a missed shot and offensive possession or from defensive efforts of the oppositions in stopping the fast attack until the regular pattern commences. This time interval may range in length from three to ten seconds, according to our research. Spreading this accumulated time over the full game means that several minutes of a game may be wasted doing nothing but making the transition from the ending of the break until the beginning of the pattern. This time interval should be used to the advantage of the offensive team. Consequently, we have developed an offense geared to take care of this interim period of time. I call this the Transitional Free-Lance Scoring Attack.

TRANSITIONAL FREE-LANCE FOUNDATION

Transitional refers to the element of time between the collapse of the fast break and the start of the formal pattern. *Free-lance* means the general techniques and methods used to move in for a shot and score. *Free-lance* does not really mean all individual movements disregarding coordination with the total team. It is a specific set of movements and plays designed for making an offensive thrust. Some of the free-lance plays are similar to other offensive moves used, while others are strictly individual movements coordinated with total team movements. This means that one player may be cutting or two players may be slashing while the other players anticipate the plays and look to fulfill a role. The role may be rebounding or defensive protection.

The Transitional Free-Lance Scoring Attack has been very useful in helping my teams establish a winning tradition through the years. Opponents often defensed the fast breaks, even along with all of the fast break options, as well as containing our patterned offenses, only to fall prey to the Transitional Free-Lance Attack. Very few opponents really understood that this was a definite offensive plan included in the total attack. This in essence was a third phase of offense which provided an added weapon with which to score. In some games, the Transitional scoring produced more points than the actual fast break itself.

This phase of the game usually made the offensive maneuvers

much more potent and kept pressure on the opponents' defense practically every second of ball possession. Needless to say, players must be quick thinking and physically versatile, while capable of using these assets in a team approach, to make this phase effective.

An attempt was made to reduce the responsibilities to simple basic rules to be observed. These generally center on cutters moving to the basket from three different floor positions. These positions are either from the left side of the court, the right side of the court, or from the middle court area and just behind the free-throw line.

Fast Break Review

The *fast break* is organized in the final stages in a closed tandem, or open tandem including a trailer. The closed tandem includes a left wingman, and a right wingman just outside the three-second lane. The third man is at the free-throw line area with a man wide in either corner. The fifth man remains back near mid-court for defensive protection. In the open tandem, the players are basically in a similar alignment, except that the wingmen's distances are different in relation to the basket. The wingmen stay out wide, near the corner, while the trailer is in close to the three-second lane. In the closed tandem, the trailer moves behind a wingman for a possible pass and shot, while in the open tandem, the trailer moves inside the wingman. In either case, at the conclusion of the break there are three players in a row up front parallel to the baseline, and a player near the foul line. The other player stays back on defense, usually near the top of the circle and on either side.

The fast break is similar to most conventional breaks except for the difference in movements after the initial break is halted. It is easy to continue the offensive flow into the Transitional attack. This is accomplished with the ball being in the hands of the player at the free-throw line. He may possess the ball as the center man on the break, since the object is to move the ball to the center area, or by way of a pass to the player in that area if the attack has been stopped with another player possessing the ball.

Of course there may be times when there is no occasion to use the Transitional, at which time there are two choices. First, the players may move into a balance wheel, since it is always available whenever the players are scrambled in the offensive end, or second, players can use the traditional methods of just setting up one of the options and starting the pattern attack. The important factor to remember is always to look for the Transitional Free-Lance Offense first before proceeding to either of the other two possibilities.

A point of importance: the player considered to be the ball handler and feeder seldom has an opportunity to become the scorer. One of the other players will be the real scoring threat, particularly the big players, since they are moving to the basket preparing to assume their positions, and are usually in ideal cutting and slashing positions. Another point to consider is that the offense starts when the ball handler passes the ball laterally and parallel to the free-throw line to another player. This is the key triggering the start.

TRANSITIONAL IDENTIFICATION CHART

Another more concise explanation of the Transitional Attack in regard to identification and time allotment can be depicted in the Transitional Identification Chart. The object of the chart is to specifically define team position of the ball and the various options available during the offensive progress. Each situation is outlined and followed to completion of the offensive thrust. Also included is the exact order of the three different offensive phases. The chart shows the development of the offense starting with defense until there is a lost ball, a score off the break, or the commencing of a pattern.

Diagram 12-1 shows the chart. At the top is the defensive aspect. Lines are drawn showing the seven basic different ways of gaining possession of the ball. They follow a violation, a ball handling turnover, a missed free throw, a missed shot, a successful shot, a successful free throw, and a jump ball. From that point, "all systems are go" for the fast break to commence. There are various ways to develop the break in accordance with each situation. Lines on the chart are drawn from ball possession to the fast-break phase. After the fast break has originated, one of two things may take place if the break is carried to conclusion. Either there will be shot attempt or there will be no shot available, with the latter due to the defense stopping the break. All of this hinges on ball possession up to this point. If a shot is attempted, the optional possibilities are a made shot, lost possession, or a shot missed but possessed. Then the next phase would be the Transitional Free-Lance Attack. If there is still no shot available, we enter the set pattern play. Articulation should be smooth from one phase to the next

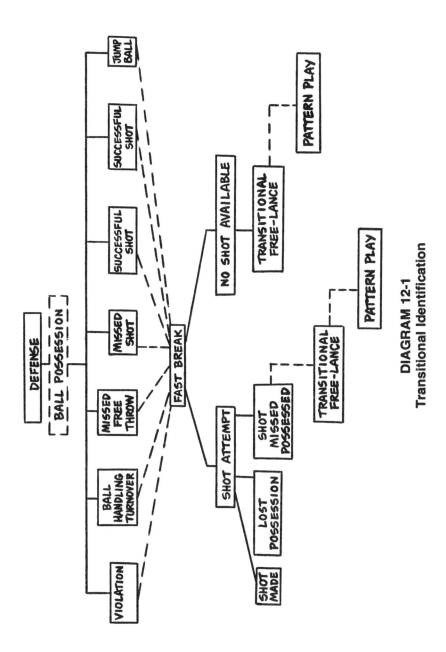

DIAGRAM 12-1
Transitional Identification

with plays geared to place players in the proper positions for one of the options to commence.

On the other hand, if no shot was available, the Transitional Free-Lance Attack is started. After this, if no shot is available, then the pattern begins.

The chart draws out the exact progression of the three phases, with each phase following in proper succession. Although the balance wheel attack is not shown on the chart, it is developed efficiently and easily from any scrambling of the offensive attack.

Ideally, the Transitional Free-Lance Attack should be used as often as possible. Following are nine basic plays perfected for the attack. It takes time to coordinate the movements, and it has been found more desirable to start with one or two basic plays and keep adding the others over the course of the season. The plays may be designated prior to the game, at halftime, or during time-outs.

Safety Man Cuts

The first series of plays and outs originates from the safety man's position at the top of the circle. He is usually the last man up court, and plays take place in the middle-court lane. In Diagram 12-2, we see an example of one safety man out. Player 1 is the ball handler with the ball at the free-throw line area. Two and 3 set up the wing positions, and 4 was the trailer in the outside position. Regardless of whether the closed tandem or open is used, the offense starts from an open tandem position. The reason for this is to make more room under the basket. In

DIAGRAM 12-2
Transitional Free-Lance Safety Man Cut

Diagram 12-2, the play continues with 2 moving up to receive the ball from 1 parallel to the free-throw line extended, while 3 and 4 move away from the basket. Five makes a sudden cut for the basket to receive a pass from 2 and a shot.

The next safety man cut play is similar, with one variation as shown in Diagram 12-3. The ball is passed by 1 to the side with the two players, 3 and 4, in this case to player 3. Five breaks in for the shot, after receiving a pass from 3, while 2 moves away from the basket, as does 4.

A third variation from the top safety man cut is shown in Diagram 12-4. In this case 3 and 4 clear out to the left side, while 2 moves up for a pass from 1. Then 2 passes to 5, who is cutting to the basket. Often 3

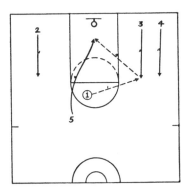

DIAGRAM 12-3
Transitional Free-Lance Safety Man Cut (*Variation*)

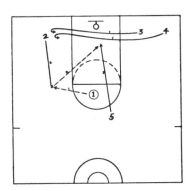

DIAGRAM 12-4
Transitional Free-Lance Wingmen Clear-Out and Safety Man Cut

or 4 may be clear for short jump shots whenever the defensive players
are slow to react due to jamming the lanes to protect against cutters.

In the final cut from the top, the safety man becomes involved in
the passing part of the play and then a weak-side crash takes place.
Diagram 12-5 shows 1 passing the ball to 5. Meanwhile, 2 and 4 move

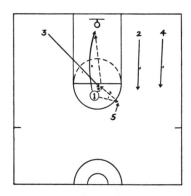

DIAGRAM 12-5
Transitional Free-Lance Safety Man Weak-Side Slash

away from the basket. Three moves to the free-throw line area for a
pass from 5 and 1 cuts for the basket and receives a pass from 3. The
side is usually wide open, and often the defender against 1 turns his
head to watch the pass to 5 and loses view of 1, allowing him to slip to
the basket.

Two-Man Slashes

Slashes can be set up and used from either the top position or a
wing position—especially since the alignment and movements of the
players are conducive to slashing type movements, with players moving towards the free-throw line away from the basket. There are more
situations which deceive the defensive players. The screen possibilities
are more prevalent from this movement.

In Diagram 12-6, the safety man slashes off either one of the two
players on the right side to open up scoring opportunities between
himself and one of the screening players. In this play, 5 darts to the
right side and breaks off either screener 3 or 4, who has moved away
from the basket into screening position. Five can break either to the left
off 3 or to the right off 4, then move to the basket. The screener then

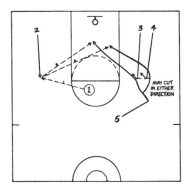

DIAGRAM 12-6
Transitional Free-Lance Safety Man—Wing Man Slash

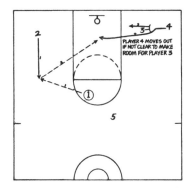

DIAGRAM 12-7
Transitional Free-Lance Wing Men Side Slash Play

rolls to the basket for a move-in play. Meanwhile 2 passes to 5 or to the open screener, rolling down if 5 is not clear.

Diagram 12-7 depicts the movement in a side slash play. One passes to 2, while 3 sets a screen for 4, who moves either right or left off 3 in the lane for a shot. Three can move after 4 moves out if he doesn't get clear. Five stays back on defense, or he can move to the backboard to assume a rebounding position.

Transitional Weave

A weave movement can also be used in the Transitional Free-Lance offense to add to the effectiveness of the attack by creating possibilities to take either a lay-up or a short jump shot. The weave theory of handing the ball off and moving in front of a defensive man and then breaking to the basket confuses the man-for-man defense. The handoff by the dribbler should be made from an inside position. The dribbler should be on the inside closest to the basket, and the receiver on the outside closer to the free-throw line.

In Diagram 12-8, the weave is demonstrated. The ball is passed to 1 starting the offense, while 5 moves from the outside position across

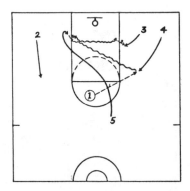

DIAGRAM 12-8
Transitional Free-Lance Three Man Weave

the lane to the low post position opposite the ball. Four then dribbles left across the lane and hands off to 3. The weave continues until there is a jump shot or a lay-up. Caution here must be taken to avoid getting caught in the three-second lane for a violation. The weave may start outside the three-second area, then move in for shot. The shot should take place easily within the allotted three-second time limit.

Criss-Cross Slashing

Often during the fast-break pattern, it is possible to end up with only three men in the fast-break tandem positions. This is because of the delay by a bigger player in moving into the break. Due to this extensive delay, the defense takes control. This can be combatted also and converted into an excellent opportunity for Transitional Free-Lance scoring. The following two examples will bear out the thought in mind.

In Diagram 12-9, three players, 1, 2, and 3 are in the triangular tandem position. One has the ball, then 1 passes the ball to 3, while 4

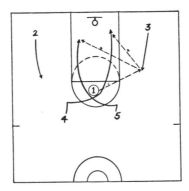

DIAGRAM 12-9
Transitional Free-Lance Criss-Cross

and 5 make a *rub-off criss-cross* movement off 1. Four fakes and breaks first, then 5 fakes and follows. Three can pass the ball to 4 or 5 for the shot. Meanwhile, 2 moves back toward the top of the circle, and 1 could either move in for a pass and shot or back on defense.

One other play from the same alignment is shown in Diagram 12-10. This is the *scramble play,* and it differs from the rub-off in that the criss-crossing takes place between 1 and the basket. This can cause confusion to the defensive players, and they often screen each other out of position. In this play, 1 passes to 3, while 5 breaks to the basket first, and 4 cuts right off 5 for the pass. Five is the inside cutter and 4 is the outside cutter. Three may become a rebounder, and 2 moves away from the basket to a defensive position.

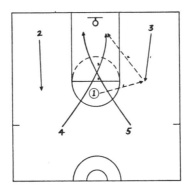

DIAGRAM 12-10
Transitional Free-Lance Scramble Play

The series of plays under discussion take considerable practice, but after being learned, they fall into a natural pattern with players reacting to each other according to the proper play. Most cuts and slashes evolve automatically—particularly when players are familiar with their teammates' moves. Since the objective in teaching the fundamentals is to give each player similar movements, it is easier to be more accurate in identifying and correlating the play sequence with the individual moves.

The Transitional Scoring Free-Lance plays are practiced as part of the fast-break drills. In fact, the drills are designed to include that attack. The writer enthusiastically endorses the value of this attack to take advantage of the interim time. It has been appreciated by coaches and teams taking the time to add this phase to their offensive system.

COACHING GUIDELINES

1. Spread out the fast-break tandem by moving out toward the sidelines if there is no shot available off the break.
2. Pass the ball at least once prior to starting the attack with a cutter or slasher. Usually the pass is from the ball handler, or point man, to another player on either side.
3. The big men should be the scoring threats rather than the point man in this attack.
4. Each player should make a move perpetuating the attack and complementing the other players rather than moving on an individual basis to develop a play.
5. If a player gets tied up with the ball, breaking up the continuity of the attack, other players move to help him release the ball to one of them. Be alert to make a quick pass to still another player close to the basket, especially since floor positions make allowances for this play.
6. Practice the Transitional Free-Lance Attack along with the fast-break drills and learn to make the progression from the fast break to the Transitional Free-Lance to the pattern attacks smoothly.
7. Look for the Transitional Free-Lance Attack in tight ball games to gain an advantage. Too often teams either force fast-break shots or take too long to set up the pattern. Consequently, they lose the ball or waste time, thus upsetting offensive effectiveness.

13

Systematized Drills
for the Cut-and-Slash

To install the Cut-and-Slash attack properly involves cooperation between the coach and the players, as well as between the players themselves. Teamwork in practices and in games between the persons involved is absolutely essential for a successful program and in implementing this fast-moving type of offense. The fun of learning to work together can be a gratifying experience for both players and coaches. Cooperation is necessary in teaching by the coach and in learning by the players. The coach must design drills which offer the players an opportunity to develop individual physical ability and a kinesthetic awareness of the immediate game situation. Then there should be drills which help blend players with these abilities into the desired offensive system.

The Cut-and-Slash system is complex in structure but simple in nature. There are a considerable number of play situations, but the plays involved are natural to the game of basketball, consequently making it possible to learn the total system readily. The key is the type of drills designed to practice, the method of practicing these drills, and the time spent practicing the selected drills.

The drills should be designed to develop the individual into a versatile and well-rounded player—or, as referred to in basketball terms, a "complete player." Another factor behind drilling should be to use those drills which have significance and pertain to the offensive makeup. Each drill should be a skill or fundamental involved in a part of the offense. The players should realize how the skill fits into the offensive plan. Most players drill hard for self-improvement when they can realize the significance of the drill to the offense.

The coach must set up a situation where quantitative learning and qualitative learning may take place, but more emphasis should be placed on the latter. In the quantitative teaching, a coach lectures and draws out specific plays and fundamentals execution. In the qualitative learning, the players actually practice a skill through fundamentals and drills until capable of performing it properly by habit. Qualitative learning should be used frequently and over long periods of time in order for the player to learn to perform the skill properly at full speed.

In teaching a skill the coach must explain the movements, demonstrate them properly, and then permit the players to execute them slowly but correctly. The players then practice the skill at full speed until it is perfected. Finally, repetition over a period of time at full speed should offer each player the opportunity to learn the skill.

A successful way to develop perception of a skill by the player is to use the Imitation-Cadence drill. In this drill a coach stands in front of the players, who are standing in four equal lines. He performs the skill at slow-motion speed while the players imitate his every move. Then the action by the boys is speeded up while the coach observes and makes constructive criticism when necessary. This method may also be applied when developing team plays as well as individual skills.

DRILLING PERFORMANCE

Establishing that the Cut-and-Slash is a multiple offense with the need for numerous individual skills to fit into the many plays is important. Development of the system takes time. However, with the drills to be discussed it is possible to speed up this process of learning the complete offense. This is particularly true after initially installing the attack, especially if the drills and parts of the offense are taught to the players beginning on the junior varsity level. It is pertinent to keep in mind that the player should develop versatility and learn how and when to use his abilities in executing the plays.

Athletes will improve skills if a sense of accomplishment accompanies their efforts. The practice should be well-planned and interesting. If goals are to be reached, there should be a balance of drills for individual skills and drills for competitive skills. Players should have fun striving to attain individual and team challenges. The athletes should be in agreement with the goals set. An adequate period of time to study and experiment with the techniques is essential, followed by actual drill and performance in the motor skills.

OVERLEARNING THEORY

Learning through drills should incorporate the overlearning approach. In this approach, the players practice a fundamental or team maneuver excessively until they can perform either skillfully.

Many coaches believe in teaching few offensive team maneuvers and spend excessive time overlearning them. It is feasible and practical to learn many offensive maneuvers utilized by the more knowledgeable basketball players of today. Without doubt, the team with players learning many maneuvers has a distinct advantage. This is possible, but it is important to include drills of the multiple nature. For example, this means that an effective skill drill must include several individual skills. The effective drill would include, for example, several skills like passing, dribbling, rebounding, and shooting.

The drills should generally be executed over the full court rather than just half the court. The more distance a player moves, the more actual work performed. If a player uses drills involving more skills over a larger playing area, overlearning is possible in less time.

THE WHOLE-PART METHOD

This is still an excellent way to help players learn to play basketball, and it can be effective in teaching the Cut-and-Slash attack. The Whole-Part method is based on practicing the complete skill or maneuver, then breaking it down into parts and practicing each part until learned, then returning to implementing the whole part. Early in the season during pre-season drills, the part system is used extensively, but as the season progresses it is more practical to learn more on the whole method. Even late in the season, it is wise occasionally to spend some practices on certain parts of skills or plays, but for the most part the practices should focus on the whole.

Early in the season, the emphasis is upon individual player development. Then the play development should be prominent. Learning offensive steps and options is more practical.

ISOLATION METHOD

Still another method to be used is one where a certain part of skill or play is practiced with emphasis on psychological concentration and psycho-motor practice. This method borrows from both the whole and the part method idea. The Isolation method permits a player to improve upon a particular skill weakness while really practicing the whole fundamental. For example, if a player were having difficulty with his elbow moving laterally from his body on the jump shot instead of staying squared to his body and pointed toward the basket, the player would then practice his jump shot but concentrate on keeping his elbow in the proper position while still performing the total shot.

This technique was first tried at Windsor University after I learned it from Jerry Stencil, an excellent golf teacher currently at the St. Clair Country Club in St. Clair, Michigan. Jerry taught new golf students the golf swing by showing the grip first, then allowing them to swing at the ball any way they could for a week. The following week he would teach the next fundamental with the emphasis upon that particular one. The focus was taken off the grip, which was learned after the over-practice in between the lessons. This procedure was followed for several weeks until the total swing was learned. Then if a golfer was having trouble with his backswing, Jerry would have him concentrate his practice on the proper take-back but complete the full swing.

This method of teaching improves parts of the fundamental and can be extremely helpful in teaching a skill properly while also improving a weak part of a skill. The isolation method is that of practicing the weak part while performing the whole skill.

DEVELOPING VERSATILITY

The drills will be explained according to two major domains that are necessary. In the first domain will be the drills used to develop individual and combined basic fundamentals, and the second domain will include drills for pattern play and total team coordination. To be the well-rounded, complete player is the goal set for players in the Cut-and-Slash attack. The following drills can help attain this goal. Drills are alternated at times to maintain enthusiasm throughout the season. The emphasis moves from excessive individual work to excessive pattern work as the season progresses. Many of the warm-up drills accentuate individual and fundamental pattern practice, which serves both purposes if used as the season progresses.

TOUGHNESS AND CONDITIONING

Basketball players should learn to absorb body contact and physical aggression during a basketball game. This takes place often and is prevalent in the slashing steps of the Cut-and-Slash Attack. This must be practiced to prevent a player from changing his style of play if excessive contact takes place. The best conditioner for absorbing contact is to encourage basketball players to participate in the football program in high school. Football is a sport predicated on players being knocked down and getting up again while absorbing physical contact. This can be very helpful to a basketball player since there are times when a player may be diving for loose balls, rebounding, or setting screens for teammates. For players lacking experience in football or any other contact sport, the coach may use the following drills to toughen up the players. These are generally used early in the season and may also be sued for conditioning drills. General conditioning otherwise is achieved with the use of fast-break or pattern drills. Plain running or exercising is practically nonexistent.

1. *Up and At Him.* All players line up in five lines. One player acts as a leader and faces the group. They follow him as he runs, performs a stunt, and bounces up to resume running in place. The leader may:

   — Fall backward and bounce up.
   — Fall backward and roll once right or left.
   — Fall frontward and bounce up.
   — Fall frontward and roll over once, either right or left, and bounce up.
   — Fall backward and make a backward somersault and bounce up.
   — Fall on his stomach, make a forward somersault, and bounce up.

2. *Bull in the Ring.* Several players get into one of the circles on the floor. On a signal, they try to bump each other out of the circle. The last one in the ring is the winner. Players should

learn to stay low with feet spread apart. In a variation of this drill the players may hop instead of having both feet on the ground.

3. *Spread-Eagle*. Players jump up as high as possible, holding their outspread legs at a 90-degree angle with their body. This should be repeated ten times.

4. *Chest Kick*. Players jump up as high as possible and kick their chest with their knees ten times. They should keep bouncing rather than stop after each jump. May also jump facing a partner and try to get up higher than the partner.

5. *Splits*. The same as above, except one leg should be forward and one leg back (ten times, alternating each foot forward).

6. *Situps*. Knees bent, as many times as possible for a given time limit.

7. *Pushups*. Fingertip pushups, trying to make as many as possible within a given time limit.

Ball Possession Drills

Players should learn to possess the basketball without panicking if a defensive player tries to take it away.

1. *Take-It-Away*. Two players grab the basketball with their hands. On a signal, each tries to take the ball. Both must establish a pivot foot. The player getting the ball is the winner.

2. *Keep-Away*. One player possesses the ball and establishes a pivot foot. The second player tries to take it away from him. The player with the ball tries to protect the ball with his body and hand movements. He should not move until the defensive man commits himself.

3. *Dribble-Away*. Same as above, except that a player dribbles the ball. He cannot move the pivot foot.

4. *Escape the Trap*. A player possesses the ball in a corner and is trapped by two defensive players. The offensive man must possess the ball for three seconds, then make a successful pass out of the trap to a teammate 15 feet away.

Shooting Drills

All of the plays learned and skills refined are useless if the ball cannot be put into the hoop. Therefore, the shooting skill should be worked at until each player is proficient in shooting and scoring with proper shots from the proper spots. He should be able to shoot an assortment of lay-ups, flip shots, hook shots, the turn-around jumpers in close, and the jump shots from outside. He should be able to shoot off the dribble, and behind a screen from outside. In addition, he should be able to use fakes prior to both close-in and outside shots. Quickness of release, fingertip control, lightness of the shot, and eyes on target (circle inside of rim) are important fundamentals to learn.

1. *Dribble-Out-and-In.* A player starts the drill from the free-throw line by dribbling in for a lay-up shot, then rebounds his own shot and dribbles out to the free-throw line, changes hands, dribbles in quickly and shoots a different lay-up, rebounding his shot and repeating the previous maneuvers until he makes ten baskets. He is developing skill in dribbling, driving, shooting, and rebounding with this drill.

2. *Pivot Man Out-and-In.* This is a similar drill to the one above except that a pivot man moves to a high post position, comes to a jump stop, receives a pass from a player about 15 feet away, executes a turn to face the basket, then dribbles in as fast as possible and shoots a lay-up, rebounds the shot, and passes the ball out to the other player. The post man repeats the same procedure until he makes ten baskets. For variety he can move to different post positions.

3. *Jump Shot and Two.* All players may use this drill, but it can be especially helpful for big players to learn to follow their shot. The player shoots a jump shot at the free-throw line, then follows the shot and retrieves the ball before it hits the ground and shoots a right-handed lay-up and follows with a left-handed lay-up.

4. *Left-to-Right.* This drill develops the hook shot for players, and particularly for the big man. A player stands under the basket facing the backboard. He shoots a short right-handed hook shot, then retrieves the ball and shoots a left-handed hook shot. He alternates hands until he makes ten baskets. A variation may be added with the player facing the middle of the court and shooting off the board from that position.

5. *Crib-Time.* A player stands under the basket and is given one minute to make as many close-in shots as possible. He should

not repeat a shot until trying at least three different ones in succession.

6. *Feed-the-Shooter.* One player is the jump shooter from outside and the other is a retriever. The retriever keeps feeding the shooter until 25 shots are taken. Then the two switch roles. The shooter should move to a different spot for each shot. This should be continued until each takes 50 shots. The player making the most baskets is the winner.

7. *Full-Court Lay-Up.* See Diagram 13-1. A player shoots at one basket, then runs to rebound at the opposite one. He then

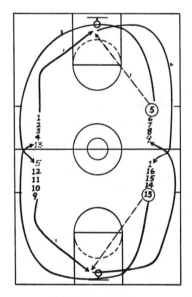

DIAGRAM 13-1
Full-Court Lay-Up Drill

returns to shoot at the original basket again and continues this procedure. For example, player 5 passes to 1 for the shot at basket A. Then 1 runs to join the rebounders at basket B. After rebounding and passing to a shooter at that basket, 1 returns to his original line, ready to shoot at basket A. To rotate shooting and rebounding assignments, the players switch lines from one sideline to the other but leave the ball there. As many as 24 players may warm up quickly with this drill.

8. *Three-Man-Cross and All Pass*. This drill is shown in Diagram 13-2. Two passes the ball to post man 5, then he and 1 criss-cross off the post. Player 5 passes the ball to 2 near the basket; 2 then passes to 1 on the other side of the basket and 1 passes to 5 moving in for the lay-up. All may rebound a missed shot and put it in.

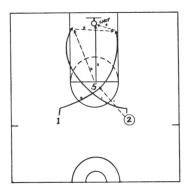

DIAGRAM 13-2
Three-Man-Cross and All Pass Drill

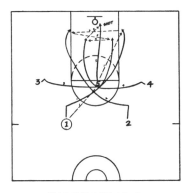

DIAGRAM 13-3
Five-Man-Cross and All Pass Drill

9. *Five-Man-Cross and All Pass*. This drill may be seen in Diagram 13-3. It is similar to the above drill, except that the four outside players cross off the post man and all four players handle the ball, with five taking the shot.
10. *Screen-and-React*. In this drill, two players work together

with one being a shooter and the other being a rebounder, passer, and screener. The screener flip-passes off to the shooter, who shoots behind the screen. The screener moves to the basket, rebounds the shot, and dribbles out to a new position within 20 feet of the basket. The shooter then fakes a cut move to the basket and drops behind the screener to receive the flip pass and shoot again. Following are some variations with this drill. The shooter may:

—Fake a drive and shoot.
—Fake a shot and drive.
—Fake a jump shot and jump pass to the screener, rolling in
   to the basket.
—Dribble off the screener and jump shoot behind him.
—Dribble off the screener and pass off on a move-in.

11. *Suicide*. This drill is made up of faking, shooting, dribbling, and rebounding. Three players are ready to play until one makes three baskets. Action is continuous and shots must be taken in the deep internal zone. The coach shoots the ball, then whichever player gets the rebound tries to score while the other two try to stop him. The player rebounding the ball tries to shoot. The first player to score three baskets is the winner. Fouling should be kept to a minimum. Offensive players must be tough, and they must be forced to use fakes and an assortment of shots. This drill also serves as an excellent toughening up exercise.

Offensive Rebounding

Skill must be developed in both securing position for rebounding and tipping the ball into the basket. The tip should be at the peak of the player's jump, and it should be with the natural hand or the one with the palm facing the basket without twisting the hand. Fingertip control is important for better touch.

1. *Basket Tap*. A player stands to the side of a basket and tips the ball off the backboard several times, then tips it into the basket. The right hand should be used from the right side and the left from that side.
2. *Circle-and-Repeat*. Five players stand to the side of the basket. The first man jumps up and lays the ball off the back-

board. The second player then jumps up and taps the ball off the board. Each player follows suit. After tipping the ball, the players circle to the end of the line ready to tap again when their turn arrives. On a signal by the coach, a tap is attempted to score.

3. *Set-Him-Up.* A player on one side of the basket tosses the ball up over the basket and off the backboard. The second player seeks to jump up and tap it into the hoop.

4. *Dribble-and-Tap.* See Diagram 13-4. Five players stand at mid-court in a line facing a basket. The first player dribbles

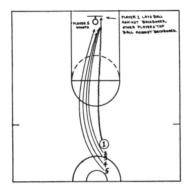

DIAGRAM 13-4
Dribble-and-Tap Drill

and lays the ball off the board. The other players follow him, and the second in line taps it back up again for the third man to follow suit. Player 5 tries to tap it into the basket. If he misses, any of the other players may tap it in. The drill ends when the basket is made.

Individual Drive Moves

The wide-open tactics used to properly implement the Cut-and-Slash offense make it apparent that each player should be capable of taking the ball to the basket with the dribble. Sometimes this is set up with a drive move from a stationary position, as off the balance wheel, and other times driving to the basket originates off a dribbling situation where the player with the ball just continues to take the ball to the basket as in the fast-break front-court tandem. Essentially, the player must be able to handle the ball well enough to get by his defensive opponent and move to the basket. He must stay low, be perceptive for a pass or shot, and have judgment as to the appropriate action.

1. *Five Spots*. Diagram 13-5 depicts the five spots the players may use to learn how to drive from a stationary position. Player 1 receives a flip pass from a defensive man to start the

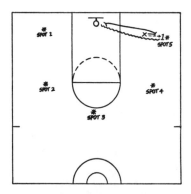

DIAGRAM 13-5
Five Spots Drill

   drill. He tries to elude his man and score with a close-in shot. If he succeeds, then he gets another try. When 1 misses a shot and the defensive man possesses the ball, the defender goes to offense and 1 goes to defense. After each has possessed the ball once, the play moves over to the next spot and the same rules are used. The spots are strategically located to familiarize the players with the court area on either side of the basket.

2. *Baseline Drive*. Diagram 13-6 shows that drill. Player 1 is under the basket. Two drives to the basket along the right baseline and takes any lay-up shot, while 3 waits out toward the corner. After the shot, 1 approaches 3 at half-speed and allows 3 to drive right or baseline for a lay-up shot. After the shot, 2 rebounds and gives passive defense to 1, driving from the corner for the shot. Each player continues to rotate to the new floor position and assumes the new role.

3. *Control-Reaction*. This drill tends to build offensive reaction by a dribbler to the defensive man. If the defense does *this*,

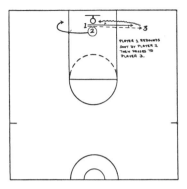

DIAGRAM 13-6
Baseline Drive Drill

DIAGRAM 13-7
Control-Reaction Drill

the offensive player does *that,* with a player beginning his dribble from 15 feet from the top of the free-throw circle. A defensive man stands at the free-throw line. The dribbler moves directly at the defensive man. The defensive player may play him to the right side, to the left side, or fake and drop back. The offensive player controls the ball and retains the balance necessary to react to do the opposite thing. For example, if he is apprehended on his right, then he switches hands from a right-hand dribble and drives in left-handed for the shot. The opposite takes place if the pressure is on the left. If the defensive man drops back, then the offensive man stops abruptly and takes the jump shot. (See Diagram 13-7.)

4. *Inside Advantage.* This is a drill with two offensive players

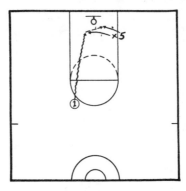

DIAGRAM 13-8
Inside Advantage Drill

trying to score near the basket against one defender. The drill
is shown in Diagram 13-8. One dribbles to the left of the
basket for a shot attempt. If the defensive man tries to guard
him, then 1 passes off to his teammate, 5.

Pattern Breakdown Drills

A breakdown of the pattern into drills which resemble parts of the
total attack is vital to achieving the second part of the reason behind
drilling. After individual development occurs, well-rounded players
then must be fitted into the team system. Learning the basic movements of the attack is essential, followed by practicing the patterns
often to help each player learn the intricacies of each option against the
various defenses. The drills to be spelled out are used with the intention of learning the principles of offense movement pertinent and
unique to the Cut-and-Slash Attack. The offensive maneuvers are not
necessarily used only in this attack, but rather are common to basketball. The organization and use of these maneuvers form the system.

Fast-Breaking Drills

This part of the offense is of prime importance because the fast
break is used as an individual attack and the fast-break alignment is
used in several parts of the attack. Much of the Cut-and-Slash relies
upon the front-court fast-break alignment. This means that the patterns
terminate the thrust in this type of organization, making it necessary to

practice the fast break frequently, both in totality and in the terminal stage. The main objective in the complete fast break is to get the ball away from the defensive boards, move up court quickly, and then set up and organize patterns to outnumber the defense. In the terminal stages, reference is to only the front-court alignment. The Transitional Free Lance Attack may also be practiced from some of these patterns.

1. *The Three-Man Weave and Break.* This drill is shown in Diagram 13-9 with the purpose being to condition the players, to learn the weave movement, and to set up the closed tandem in the front-court. Player 4 starts the drill by passing to 7, then following his pass. Seven passes to 1 coming toward the middle of the court. This passing continues with the passer going behind the receiver, heading toward a sideline, then cutting back toward the middle for a pass. The player receiving the ball just over the ten-second line dribbles to the free-throw line. Meanwhile, his two partners assume a wing position in the tandem. The ball handler passes off to a wingman or shoots a jumper himself. The

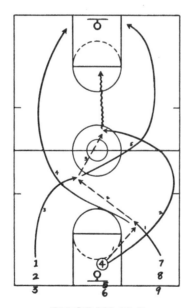

DIAGRAM 13-9
Three-Man Weave and Break Drill

players can also practice an open tandem from this drill. They then retrieve the shot and repeat the drill back to the original basket.

2. *The Five-Man Weave and Break.* This drill is similar to the previous one with the following exceptions: Five players weave to a point just over mid-court to set up the front-end alignment with the trailer and safety man. The Transitional Free-Lance Attack can be practiced from this drill. The drill is shown in Diagram 13-10.

3. *Speed-Up.* Quickness and speed may be worked on in this drill and can be particularly helpful to big players. Diagram 13-11 shows the drill. Tall player 4 passes the ball to small player 1 at mid-court; then 4 breaks full speed for the far basket. Player 1 passes long to 4 for the lay-up shot. The same procedure is followed with 4 returning for the shot at the original basket.

4. *Finish It Right.* This is a half-court drill setting up the front-end fast-break alignment. Both tandems and all of the innovations may be practiced from this drill. In Diagram 13-12, a wide tandem is formed. Player 7 dribbles to the foul line.

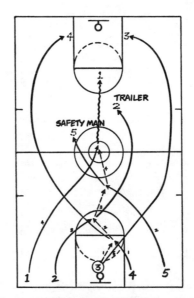

DIAGRAM 13-10
Five-Man Weave and Break Drill

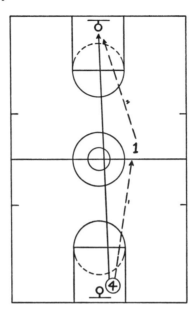

DIAGRAM 13-11
Speed-Up Drill

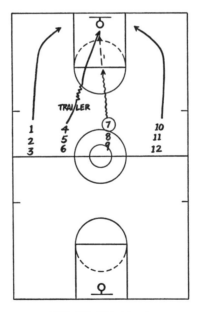

DIAGRAM 13-12
Finish-It-Right Front-End Fast-Break Alignment Drill

Trailer player 4 receives a pass from dribbler 7 for an easy shot. Players 1 and 10 are wingmen.

5. *Action Line*. Often players don't react as a unit in changing from defense to offense. Still other times a player tries to prevent the ball from bouncing out of bounds by a supreme effort, only to have his teammates standing out of position watching the play instead of helping him out by moving to receive his pass. In this drill, players learn to react to a loose-ball situation. In Diagram 13-13, the coach lobs the

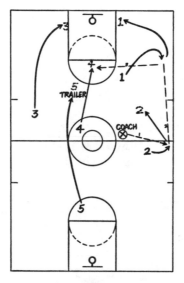

DIAGRAM 13-13
Action-Line Drill

ball toward the sideline and points to a basket indicating which way the offensive team must move. Player 2 retrieves the loose ball and passes to 1 deep in the offensive court on the right side. Then 1 passes to 4 at the free-throw line while the other players fill in the appropriate positions for a front-end alignment and shot. If a player is near the basket, he may shoot and not wait for the formation of the alignment. Also, a useful innovation is not to permit any dribbling. This also helps players learn body control and stopping along with alertness and team work. The drill can originate from any-where on the court.

Cutting

Any practice in cutting should include some time to be spent on faking and starting. Timing is essential in cutting, as is quick starting.

1. *Two-on-Two All-Purpose.* The various cuts and screen plays can be tried off this drill. (See Diagram 13-14.) Two players,

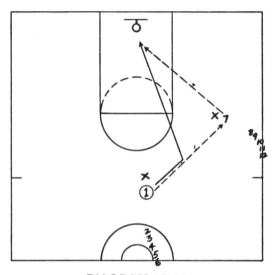

DIAGRAM 13-14
Two-on-Two All-Purpose Drill

1 and 7, play two-man basketball against the two defensive men. In this diagram, 1 passes to 7, moves toward him, then breaks up the middle for a return pass from 7 and a shot. Other plays to be tried are:

—Pass and screen for 7.
—Dribble toward 7 for a screen and role play.
—A clear-out by 7, and a drive by 1.
—A pass to 7, then a return pass to 1 behind 7's screen for a
   jump shot by 1.

After possession by the defense, players 1 and 7 then go on defense, while 2 and 8 become the offensive players. Meanwhile, the two defensive players get into the offensive line to await a turn.

Slashing Drills

At least three players must work together in the drills to practice slashing. A player slashing must be alert to fake before running an opponent into the screener if this is necessary.

1. *Hook-Up and Go*. See Diagram 13-15. Player 5 sets a screen and faces the basket to the left of the three-second lane. Player 3 fakes, then hooks his defensive opponent off on 5 and heads for the foul line as player 5 moves to the basket. At this time, 1 looks either to 3 for a jump shot, or to 5 for a close-in shot. Of course, 5 is preferred.

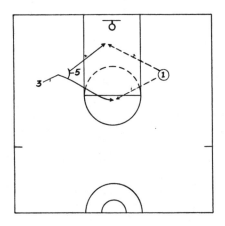

DIAGRAM 13-15
Hook-Up and Go Drill

2. *Rub-Off and Go*. This drill is based on a theory similar to that of the previous play except that 5 may have his back to the basket when setting the screen. In Diagram 13-16, player 1 passes to 2, then cuts off 5 to the basket. Meanwhile, 5 rolls in after 1 cuts. A pass to 1 is the first possibility, and a pass to 5 is the alternate.

Balance Wheel Drills

Quick jump shots are possible off the wheel, as are quick passes to the low post man and a drive by any player receiving a pass. The players must react quickly to the most suitable possibility. Other drills

DIAGRAM 13-16
Rub-Off and Go Drill

mentioned for driving and shooting help prepare the players for these moves, but the following drill is a way of practicing the balance wheel.

1. *Balance-Wheel It.* All the offensive players move in close to the basket in any scattered formation. The coach flips the ball to a player, and then the others fill in the wheel. In Diagram 13-17, the coach flips the ball to player 3, who passes out to 1. The ball is moved on the outside to the right top spot to 2, who passes to 5 at the low post position on the right for a close-in shot.

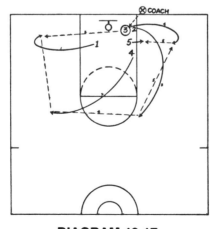

DIAGRAM 13-17
Balance-Wheel It Drill

Weak-Side Slashing Drills

The plays necessary for this maneuver can be practiced off the balance wheel formation but can also be broken down and perfected with the three-on-three play.

1.   *Three-on-Three All-Purpose.* Diagram 13-18 shows this drill. Player 1 passes to 5 at a high post. Then 5 plays three-

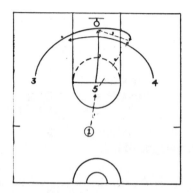

DIAGRAM 13-18
Three-on-Three All-Purpose Drill

on-three basketball with 3 and 4 against their opponents. In this diagram, 5 passes to 2 after 3 and 4 make a forward exchange. Then 5 moves to the basket for a return pass from 3 for a shot. Other plays to be practiced are:

—The double screen.
—Forwards clear-out.
—Center drop-behind.
—Center-forward screen and roll from a dribble.
—Center-forward pick and roll from a pass.

Team Patterns Drills

A team can both learn the patterns and warm up while dummying or practicing the options without a defensive team. This should be practiced often. The real live scrimmaging can then take place as mentioned earlier by running against the junior varsity team on the two side courts (if this is available). Team movement and total team action is the desire here to perfect the pattern play. The same can be tried with the pattern attack against full-court pressure.

1. *Dummy Attack.* Each option against a man-for-man half-court or full-court pressure may be practiced. Diagram 13-19 depicts players moving through a full-court pattern with no defensive opponent. Players can rotate clockwise to new starting positions after the shot is taken in order to learn play from different positions.

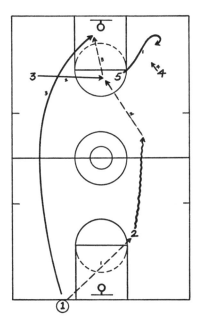

DIAGRAM 13-19
Dummy Attack Drill

2. *Multipurpose Scrimmage.* Scrimmage is important and should be used for long periods of time throughout the season. Either the half-court scrimmage or full-court scrimmage should be used. A good way to combine these two forms of scrimmaging is with the Multipurpose Scrimmage Drill. In this type of scrimmaging, team A takes possession of the ball at half-court and attacks team B with any option designated. When B team gains ball possession, players fast-break or react just as they should in a real game, moving to their

offensive basket. Team A would of course revert to defense and try to stop the attack. Then after Team B fast-breaks if they don't score in ten seconds, the scrimmaging stops. Team B will possess the ball and work an option. Even if team B had scored off the fast break, they still possess the ball at mid-court for an offensive play because team A had the previous opportunity to start the drill. Team A would defend, then fast-break as did team B. The drill can get hectic when the ball is stolen without a shot by either team. This situation is guided by the rule that a team has ten seconds to shoot after ball possession. This controlled scrimmage resembles a game but it allows the coach to change options while each team has an equal opportunity to start an offense.

COMPETITIVE GAMES

It is advantageous to practice specialties with competitive games. One such game is the two-minute contest which was described in the chapter on special situations. There are two other games which can improve specialties play that are worth explaining.

1. *Jump-Ball Game.* This game is played by two teams, the idea being to learn to react to jump ball situations at different circles and against players of different sizes. Sixteen points constitute a game. Points may be made in the following manner: The team possessing the tap receives one point. If the ball is stolen, that player's team receives a point. Upon team possession, there are five seconds to score a basket by the team possessing the ball. If a basket is made, the team receives two points. The next jump-ball situation must be played in another circle with two other players.

2. *Out-of-Bounds Underneath the Basket.* This game is played when a team takes the ball out of bounds, then tries to score within ten seconds. Points are awarded only for baskets. The ball switches hands after each play attempt, with the first team that makes 16 points winning. This game may also be used with the ball out of bounds along the sideline in the front court against a tight man-to-man defense.

PERCEPTION DEVELOPMENT

A player should become perceptive and cognizant of other players on the court. Only if he develops this perception can a player really become an effective team player. He must not only know where his own players are located on the court, but must also know the distribution of the opposition.

1. *Freeze and Point Out.* The theory behind this drill may be applied to many of the others discussed. Awareness of the situation and location of players must be practiced continually for improvement in perception. In this drill, the coach blows a whistle and all players freeze right where they are, facing straight ahead. The coach asks a player (or players) to point to teammates and opponents without turning his head. He should be able to locate them with ease. Another way is for the coach to stop a fast-break drill and question the player in regard to alternate moves or shots available. The hope is that players will become aware of play execution possibilities and also player location at all times, thus developing perception. This concept has brought excellent results with the teams coached by me and with boys attending the Summer Camp.

TOURNAMENTS

Another method in adding competition and fun in practices while helping players improve fundamentally is to plan tournaments from time to time. The tournaments should be helpful both in individual and team bases. Tournaments can be repeated, since little time is necessary for completion, such as free-throwing and shooting contests. Following are six suggestions for tournaments furthering player development:

—One-on-one tournament with 20 points constituting the winner.
—Two-on-two, 20 points to win.
—Free throwing, any designated number of baskets.
—Jump shooting, any designated number of baskets.
—Two-minute game.

Teammates and opponents should change from time to time in order to give each player the chance to compete with and against all players on the team for more interest.

A FINAL WORD FROM THE AUTHOR

As you have probably noticed, I get excited about basketball. I get very excited about the Cut-and-Slash Attack. What is it about this attack that excites me? The fact that the Cut-and-Slash meets the demands and criteria that can develop offensive maximum potential of an individual player and a team. It is a brand of basketball that offers players a chance to play the game with the most modern conceptions. This attack does justice to the player, coach, and spectator—as well as to the game itself. It is truly a completely modern attack. If anything is lacking, we will search to find it. Players must enjoy to the fullest this wonderful game of basketball.

Index